Southwest Cooking

By
June Crozier Towers

EAKIN PRESS ★ Austin, Texas

Recipes in this collection were developed by the author over a period of twenty-two years for Imperial Holly Corporation and are published in this book with permission from Imperial Holly.

FIRST EDITION

Copyright © 1991
By June Crozier Towers

Published in the United States of America
By Eakin Press
An Imprint of Eakin Publications, Inc.
P.O. Drawer 90159 ★ Austin, TX 78709-0159

ALL RIGHTS RESERVED. No part of this book may be reproduced in any form without written permission from the publisher, except for brief passages included in a review appearing in a newspaper or magazine.

ISBN 0-89015-801-0

Library of Congress Cataloging-in-Publication Data

Towers, June Crozier.
    Southwest cooking / by June Crozier Towers.
        p. cm.
        "Recipes in this collection were developed by the author over a period of 22 years for Imperial Holly Corporation."
    Includes index.
    ISBN 0-89015-801-0 (hardback) : $12.95
    1. Cookery, American — Southwestern style. I. Imperial Holly Corporation.
    II. Title.
TX715.2.S69T69   1991
641.5979 — dc20   90-40355
                                                                                           CIP

This book is dedicated to some special people who made this book possible:

My Mother, the BEST cook;

Quentin, who enjoyed experimenting with new foods;

Richard Brown, who gave me the job twenty-two years ago as Home Economics Director for Imperial Sugar;

Ann Criswell, an inspiration for twenty-two plus years;

Joan Little, Susan Wilmoth, and **Don Robertson,** who taught me "computer sense";

Betty, who proofread the manuscript;

IMPERIAL HOLLY CORPORATION for permission to use recipes I developed for Imperial's packaging, cookbooks, advertising and newspaper columns;

PAUL, DIANE, and **CHARLOTTE** who still call home for a favorite recipe; and

Friends and relatives who have shared their best recipes.

Bless you; I couldn't have done it without you!

Imperial Holly Corporation

Sugar Land, Texas, has long been the "sweetest" town in the Southwest because of the tons of raw sugar that arrive by rail each day and emerge from the Imperial refinery as the finest granulated, brown and powdered sugar available.

Sugar Land was named because of the fields of sugar cane growing in the area as early as 1843 when Imperial Sugar Company was founded. Imperial Sugar was the only mill to survive the forays of Santa Anna's army and is now the oldest Texas company doing business continuously on the same site.

This means, of course, that in 1993, Imperial Sugar, which is now Imperial Holly Corporation, will celebrate its 150th anniversary as a Texas business making life sweeter for all of the Southwest. Knowing that Imperial has a refining capacity of four million pounds of sugar a day, it's not hard to guess just what kind of sweet tooth we really have.

And now that Imperial has acquired Holly Corporation, a sugar beet refiner formerly headquartered in Colorado Springs, Colorado, there are two "sweetest" towns in Texas — the second is Hereford in far West Texas.

The recipes and jacket photographs in *Southwest Cooking* are used through the kind permission of Imperial Holly Corporation for the enhanced enjoyment of good cooks throughout the Southwest. Recipe collectors of all ages will be happy to know that about seventy-five percent of the recipes in this collection were perfected by June Towers for Imperial's packaging and cookbooks. Look for familiar recipes hiding behind new names.

Contents

Foreword

Southwesterners are friendly folks and have been since the days when survival meant pulling together to survive the perils of establishing new homes in a hostile environment. Graduating from covered wagon to dugout to log cabin, pioneers struggled to grind out an existence while envisioning a better life someday. No matter where they came from — the Southwest was settled by folks from northern and eastern states of America and about forty nations — families leaned on each other in times of illness, death, when storms swept across the prairie, when crops failed. As in the early years, the Southwest still extends a warm welcome to new neighbors, often in the form of food on moving day. Likewise, the foods imported by newcomers infuse fresh vigor into the Southwestern kitchen.

Recipes in this book are only a few that Southwesterners love to eat and share with friends — recipes that have been enjoyed, saved and passed down from generation to generation. Approximately three-fourths of these recipes were developed specifically for Imperial's packaging, so you may recognize an old favorite by another name.

Introduction

We first met over the telephone in a discussion of bunny-shaped breads for an Easter feature I was doing. I am happy to say that discussion was the beginning of an association and friendship that's still going strong more than twenty years later.

A few years after that phone conversation I was surprised to meet June on a professional level — she had prepared the foods for a color photograph for Imperial Sugar, having, through necessity, after the death of her husband, Quentin Nelson, evolved from a wife and homemaker into a woman with a career.

As is her style, she saw something that needed to be done and educated herself to do it by studying, reading and cooking with voracious enthusiasm and energy. She soon became Home Economics Director for Imperial. By that time none of her friends were so surprised because we knew June's determination and organizational skills.

Now it's time for her to share the fruits of twenty-two years of professional cooking with an appreciative audience, including many who have followed June's food columns in Fort Bend County newspapers and magazines.

You'll enjoy her practical and people-friendly recipes, but most of all you'll enjoy the great tastes.

ANN CRISWELL
Food Editor
Houston Chronicle

BREADS

Bake the Best Bread

Southwestern cooks have known for a mighty long time that the aroma of fresh-baked bread is the surest way to keep the kids close to the hearth. Nothing is more enticing than homemade bread just begging for butter and strawberry preserves. Nothing gets kids scooting for home quicker than muffins, biscuits or slices of 100% whole wheat bread made by mom. These breads are better than cake and easier to make.

You'll grin with pleasure when your kids and their friends reach for another sopapilla drenched in honey. Perhaps your young ones love hush puppies and ask over and over to hear the story about how hush puppies got their name. These crisp, crunchy, yet tender-on-the-inside delicacies were invented by dropping teaspoonfuls of cornbread into hot fat where the fish had been fried. In the early days when this was done in a large black pot outside under the oak trees, these frying nuggets just about drove the dogs crazy. Their barking was halted, momentarily, by cries of, "Hush, puppy!" Or, so the story goes.

This collection of easy and delectable breads will make your family "Southwestern" Proud!

OUACHITA APRICOT BREAD

Fresh fruits were a luxury for early Southwesterners. So dried fruits became a staple. We still cherish them eaten as snacks or in fruit and nut breads.

Yield: 1 (8" x 4" x 3") loaf.

1 cup dried apricots, chopped
1 cup Imperial Granulated Sugar
2 tbsp. shortening
1 egg, well beaten
1/2 cup orange juice

1/4 cup Imperial Granulated Sugar
2 cups all-purpose flour
2 tsp. baking powder
1/2 tsp. soda
1 tsp. salt
1 cup chopped nuts

Soak chopped apricots in water to cover for 20 minutes. Cream together the 1 cup sugar, shortening and egg. Stir in orange juice and 1/4 cup sugar. Combine dry ingredients and add to creamed mixture, blending well. Drain the apricots and stir into batter, adding nuts at the same time. Pour into greased and floured 8" x 4" x3" loaf pan. Bake in preheated 350-degree oven 65 minutes or until done. Cool on rack. To store, wrap airtight.

AMARILLO CHEDDAR BREAD

Southwestern pioneers brought their cheesemaking skills and appetites to the "wild west." British ancestors would love modern uses of their classic Cheddar cheese.

Yield: 3 (7 1/2" x 4") loaves.

4 cups all-purpose flour
2 tbsp. Imperial Granulated Sugar
1 tbsp. baking powder
1 1/2 tsp. salt
1/2 cup (1 stick) unsalted butter, cut in chunks

3 cups (8 oz.) sharp Cheddar cheese, shredded
1 tbsp. fresh dill, minced (1 tsp. if dried)
2 eggs
2 cups milk

Combine dry ingredients and cut in butter until mixture looks like meal. Stir in the cheese and dill. Whisk eggs and combine with milk; add to dough and stir just until moistened. Divide batter among 3 greased 7^1/$_2$" x 4" loaf pans. Bake in preheated 400-degree oven about 45 minutes. Cool 10 minutes in pans, then turn out onto racks and cool. Wrap in plastic wrap and store in ziplock bags.

BORDER BUTTERFLAKE BISCUITS

In the early Southwest, biscuits were a staple — for breakfast with gravy, bacon and eggs — for lunch and dinner. But they were never this light and flaky.

Yield: 24 (2") biscuits.

2 cups all-purpose flour, approximate
1 tbsp. baking powder
^{3}/$_4$ tsp. salt
1 tbsp. Imperial Granulated Sugar

^{1}/$_2$ cup (1 stick) plus 2 tbsp. butter or margarine
2 eggs, well beaten
^{1}/$_3$ cup cold milk

Combine dry ingredients until thoroughly mixed; cut butter or margarine into mixture with pastry blender or fork. Combine eggs and milk; add to first mixture and mix lightly with fork, adding more flour to make soft but not sticky dough. Shape dough into ball and turn out onto lightly floured surface. With rolling pin, lightly roll dough into rectangle about ^{1}/$_2$ inch thick. Fold dough in thirds and roll into oblong two more times. With dough ^{1}/$_2$ inch thick, cut into two-inch rounds. Or, pinch off dough, roll into balls and place in muffin tins. Bake biscuits on ungreased baking sheet in preheated 450-degree oven until biscuits are puffed and golden brown.

NOTE: For best results, handle the dough very gently, both in mixing and rolling out the dough.

MERCADO JALAPENO CORNBREAD

When wide open spaces were a way of life, a loud yell of "come and get it" meant you'd better get to the kitchen table fast for a full selection of vittles, especially the cornbread.

Yield: 9 squares.

3/4 cup yellow corn meal
1 1/4 cups all-purpose
    flour
1/4 cup Imperial
    Granulated Sugar
1/2 tsp. salt
1 tbsp. baking powder
1/2 tsp. cayenne pepper
Dash of garlic powder,
    optional

1 egg, beaten
3/4 cup milk
1/4 cup cooking oil
1 tbsp. minced onion
2 tbsp. minced jalapeno
    pepper
2 tbsp. minced pimiento
    or red bell pepper

Combine dry ingredients in large bowl and mix well with slotted spoon. Combine remaining ingredients and stir into first mixture lightly. Bake in preheated 8″ heavy cast iron or thick pottery dish containing 2 tbsp. oil or shortening. Bake in preheated 425-degree oven 20 to 25 minutes. Preheating of dish or pan produces brown, crusty bread.

CORSICANA CRUNCHY BREAD STICKS

These innovative bread sticks carry on an old Southwestern tradition — waste not, want not.

Yield: 16 bread sticks.

4 hot dog buns
1/4 cup butter or
    margarine, melted
Dash of garlic powder

1/4 tsp. Worcestershire
    sauce
Dash of Salt
Dash of white pepper or
    cayenne

Split hot dog buns in half, then cut each half vertically to make 4 bread sticks from each bun. Combine all other ingredients and brush onto cut edges of bread sticks. Place on baking sheet and brown in 325-degree oven about 10 minutes. Let remain in oven a few minutes after heat is turned off to make sticks very crisp. Delicious with drinks, salads, soups, or the main dish.

ROSENBERG CZECHFEST KOLACHES

The Southwest has always been an enriching cultural mix. Without the Czech heritage, we might have to go to Prague for these delicious sweet breads — kolaches.

Yield: about 5 dozen kolaches.

1 tsp. Imperial
   Granulated Sugar
1 pkg. dry yeast
$^1/_2$ cup lukewarm water
1 cup lukewarm milk,
   scalded and cooled
$^1/_2$ cup Imperial
   Granulated Sugar

$^1/_2$ tsp. salt
6 tbsp. ($^3/_4$ stick) butter or
   margarine, melted
2 eggs
5–6 cups all-purpose
     flour
Filling (see below)

Combine 1 tsp. sugar, yeast and water; stir and set aside. Combine remaining ingredients, except flour, and beat to blend. Gradually add enough flour to make a smooth semi-soft dough. Turn dough out onto lightly floured board; knead about 10 minutes, until elastic and shiny. Place dough in greased bowl, cover with damp cloth and let rise until doubled. When ready, punch down and pinch off balls of dough, flatten them and put filling in depression in center of each. Brush with melted butter and sprinkle with sugar. Bake in preheated 375-degree oven about 10 minutes. If desired, drizzle with powdered sugar glaze.

Prune Filling:

Cook 1 cup dried prunes in $^1/_4$ cup of water until tender; drain, cool, pit, mash and sieve. Add $^1/_2$ cup sugar, $^1/_2$ tsp. vanilla, $^1/_2$ tsp. lemon juice and sprinkle of cinnamon; reheat to blend flavors. Add cream or prune juice for proper consistency. Cool before adding to dough.

Apricot Filling:

Substitute dried apricots for dried prunes and substitute almond flavoring for the vanilla.

FIESTA APPLESAUCE BREAD

Vegetable and fruit seeds always found stowaway space during the push Westward. So fruit pies, breads and sauces became jewels of the frontier. They are still reason enough to celebrate.

Yield: 1 (9″ x 5″ x 3″) loaf

2 cups all-purpose flour
³/₄ cup Imperial
    Granulated Sugar
1 tbsp. baking powder
1 tsp. salt
¹/₂ tsp. soda
¹/₂ tsp. cinnamon

1 cup chopped pecans or
    walnuts
1 egg, slightly beaten
1 cup canned or fresh-
    made applesauce
2 tbsp. melted shortening

Combine dry ingredients; add nuts. In mixing bowl beat egg; add applesauce and shortening. Stir in dry ingredients, stirring only enough to blend ingredients. Pour into greased 9″ x 5″ x 3″ loaf pan. Bake in preheated 350-degree oven for 1 hour. Cool for a few minutes, then remove from pan and cool on rack. Wrap in plastic wrap or foil to store. Sweet breakfast idea: slice, spread with butter and broil until golden.

FOLKLIFE FESTIVAL SOPAPILLAS

Mexican settlers came north into the Southwest bringing culinary traditions like sopapillas which have become favorite food fare — especially at San Antonio's Folklife Festival.

Yield: about 1 dozen

1 cup all-purpose flour
¹/₂ tsp. salt
1 tsp. baking powder
1 tbsp. Imperial
   Granulated Sugar

¹/₂ tbsp. shortening
5 tbsp. milk
Oil for frying

Combine dry ingredients; cut in shortening and add milk to make a dough just firm enough to roll. Cover bowl and let dough stand 30 to 60 minutes. Roll dough ¹/₄ inch thick on lightly floured board; cut in diamond shapes. Heat 1 inch of oil to 375 degrees F. Electric skillet works well. Add a few pieces of dough at a time, turning once so they will puff evenly, then turn again to brown on both sides. Drain on paper towels and keep hot in warm oven. Serve with butter and honey thinned with a little water.

NOTE: Roll dough very thin and fry in very hot oil a few at a time for the puffiest sopapillas.

BRANDED PANCAKES FOR
LITTLE SOUTHWESTERNERS

Kids from three years to 103 enjoy cooking fun foods. These branded pancakes are better than a rodeo for honest-to-gosh fun.

Yield: 6 medium pancakes

1¹/₄ cups all-purpose
   flour
2 tsp. baking powder
1 tbsp. Imperial
   Granulated Sugar

¹/₂ tsp. salt
¹/₂ tsp. soda
1 egg, beaten
1¹/₄ cups buttermilk
2 tbsp. margarine, melted

Combine flour, baking powder, sugar, salt and soda together in mixing bowl and mix thoroughly. In another bowl, combine beaten egg, buttermilk and melted margarine; combine the two mixtures and stir until barely mixed. Using a teaspoon, drip batter onto hot skillet to make your personal Southwestern "brand." Cook about one minute, then add enough batter over your design to make a whole pancake. Cook until brown on the underside and bubbly on top. Turn and cook second side; don't overcook. Serve with Imperial Brown

Sugar Syrup: bring 2 cups Imperial Brown Sugar and 1 cup water to a boil; simmer for 5 minutes. Makes about 1½ cups.

NOTE: When making a brand or your initials, remember that they must be made backwards in order to be correct when the pancake is turned right side up.

METROPLEX MUFFINS

Wide-open spaces of yesteryear have merged into urban areas where city folks still enjoy hearty, basic foods like Metroplex Muffins.

Yield: 12 (2½″) muffins.

¼ cup Imperial Granulated Sugar
1½ cups all-purpose flour
2 tsp. baking powder
1 tsp. salt
1 cup quick-cooking oatmeal

1 egg, well beaten
¾ cup milk
¼ cup (½ stick) butter or margarine, melted
¼ cup molasses

Combine sugar, flour, baking powder, salt and oatmeal and mix well. Combine egg, milk, butter or margarine and molasses and add all at once to flour mixture, stirring only enough to combine without overmixing. Spoon batter into 12 (2½-inch) muffin cups. Bake in preheated 400-degree oven for about 20 minutes or until richly browned. Remove from pan at once. For variety, add chopped nuts, chocolate morsels or raisins to batter before baking.

HIGH PLAINS WHOLE WHEAT BREAD

Westward-rolling covered wagons were gradually replaced by ranchers and farmers. Endless wheat fields throughout the Southwest still supply the basic ingredient for good bread and other baked foods.

Yield: 2 loaves

$^1/_2$ cup Imperial Brown
   Sugar, firmly packed
$1^1/_2$ cups milk
$^1/_4$ cup butter or
   margarine
2 tsp. salt

2 pkgs. dry yeast
$^1/_2$ cup warm water
6 cups (approx.) whole
   wheat flour
Melted butter or
   margarine

Combine brown sugar, milk, butter or margarine and salt; heat until butter melts. Cool to lukewarm. Soften yeast in water, then stir in the lukewarm milk mixture. Stir in 5 cups of the whole wheat flour. Distribute $^1/_2$ cup flour on board or table surface and turn out dough onto the flour. With floured hands, knead dough for about 10 minutes while gradually adding more flour until dough is not sticky. Divide dough in half and shape each into a loaf. Place loaves in well-greased $8^1/_2''$ x $4^1/_2''$ loaf pans. Cover, freeze, then wrap each loaf securely; return to freezer. When ready to bake, remove freezer wrap, cover with plastic wrap and let thaw at room temperature about 2 hours. Then, let rise, covered, in a warm place about 2 hours. Brush loaves with melted butter. Bake in a preheated 375-degree oven for about 30 minutes. Cool on racks. If desired, bread may be baked in round loaves on baking sheets. Or, cover and refrigerate the loaves for several hours, let rise in warm place about 45 minutes and bake as above. Or, let rise and bake without freezing or refrigeration.

STATE FAIR HUSHPUPPIES

Every State fair gives rural folks a chance to brag about their skills and products. Hushpuppies recall the sights, sounds, and tastes of state fair days in Louisiana.

Yield: 12 large hushpuppies

$^1/_4$ cup all-purpose flour
$^3/_4$ cup corn meal
4 tsp. baking powder
1 heaping tsp. Imperial
   Granulated Sugar
$^1/_2$ tsp. each of garlic
   powder, coriander and
   chili powder

$^1/_4$ tsp. cayenne pepper
1 heaping tsp. each
   chopped parsley, green
   onion, pimiento, boiled
   shrimp and lump
   crabmeat
1 beaten egg
$^1/_2$ cup milk

Combine all ingredients in a bowl adding enough of the milk to moisten batter. Shape scant teaspoons of batter into small nuggets and drop into 365-degree F. cooking oil. Turn hushpuppies once as they brown and cook until deep golden brown. Remove from oil, drain and salt to taste.

WURSTFEST SAUSAGE ROLLS

Spicy sausage dating back to the early German immigrant days combines happily with delicate yeast bread to make delicious sausage rolls. Look for them at the New Braunfels Wurstfest.

Yield: about 36 sausage rolls

1 pkg. dry yeast or 1 cake of yeast	1 tsp. salt
2 tbsp. warm water	1 cup hot water
1 tsp. Imperial Granulated Sugar	3 eggs, beaten
$^1/_2$ cup shortening	4–4$^1/_2$ cups all-purpose flour
$^1/_2$ cup Imperial Granulated Sugar	Wurst sausage cut in 1$^1/_2$ x $^1/_2''$ strips

Combine yeast, warm water and 1 tsp. sugar; set aside. Combine shortening, $^1/_2$ cup sugar, salt, hot water and eggs; beat well. Add yeast mixture. Add 2 cups of the flour and beat well. Stir in another 2–2$^1/_2$ cups of the flour to make a soft dough. Refrigerate covered dough in large mixing bowl overnight. Divide dough into three portions; roll each into a circle $^1/_4''$ thick and cut into 2$''$ rounds. Simmer sausages in covered pan 5 minutes, then place sausages in centers of the circles of dough. Moisten edges of dough with water, lap one side of dough over sausages and press edges of dough together to seal. Repeat with remaining dough. Place rolls on greased cookie sheets and let rise about 1$^1/_2$ hours or until doubled in bulk. Bake in preheated 350-degree oven 10 to 12 minutes, or until golden brown. You'll be dancing in the kitchen to polka music from the Wurstfest.

NOTE: If desired, a portion of the dough can be baked and the rest may be refrigerated for later use for up to four days. Also, sausage may be omitted to make plain but delicious rolls.

DESSERTS

14

Dessert — the Dramatic Finish

Maybe chicken fried steak with mashed potatoes smothered in cream gravy alongside green beans straight from the garden and flavored with bacon is your idea of eating high on the hog. Most Southwesterners would agree. That is, until they get the first whiff of hot cherry cobbler paired up with vanilla ice cream fresh out of the old-fashioned ice cream freezer. Look at those grins when they see hot apple pie with tangy Cheddar cheese. Listen to folks on the range or hustlers in the board room chuckle when chocolate cake is passed around the table. Watching and listening will let you know real quick what's really important when folks of all ages and careers gather round to eat.

Here's a nostalgic collection of favorite Southwestern desserts to savor when the barbecue and potato salad, pinto beans and rice, fried chicken and blackeyed peas, vegetable soup and cornbread are wonderful memories.

Take your pick of cakes, candies, cookies, pies and miscellaneous desserts to satisfy every sweet tooth. Some recipes are old, some new; most are easy; a few are a bit more complex; all are delicious in the Southwestern tradition.

Cakes

BEEHIVE HONEY CAKES

Southwestern bees and wild flowers combine to make a unique honey that makes many foods taste better.

Yield: 12 (2″) cupcakes

1 egg, well beaten
³/₄ cup Imperial
    Granulated Sugar
1 tbsp. butter or
    margarine, melted
1 cup dairy sour cream
1 tsp. vanilla

1¹/₂ cups all-purpose
    flour
2 tsp. baking powder
¹/₄ tsp. soda
³/₄ tsp. salt
Honey Topping (see
    below)

Beat egg until frothy; beat in sugar and butter or margarine. Cream until light and fluffy. Add sour cream and vanilla; blend well. Combine dry ingredients and add to the sour cream mixture. Blend well. Pour into greased (2″) muffin tins. Bake in preheated 350-degree oven about 15 minutes or until cakes test done. Spread Honey Topping over cakes and return to oven until topping is bubbling. Serve warm.

Honey Topping:

Combine ¹/₂ cup honey, 2 tbsp. Imperial Brown Sugar, ¹/₂ tsp. cinnamon and 2 tbsp. melted butter or margarine.

NEWTON COUNTY BUTTERMILK FIG CAKE

Fig trees grow in many Southwestern backyards, and fig preserves simmer in lots of kitchens to enhance biscuits and other hot breads. And to make this delicious cake.

Yield: 1 (10″) Bundt cake

1 cup Imperial
   Granulated Sugar
1¹/₂ sticks (³/₄ cup) butter
   or margarine
4 eggs
1 tsp. vanilla
3 cups all-purpose flour
1 tsp. soda

1 tsp. nutmeg
1 tsp. cinnamon
¹/₄ tsp. salt
1 cup buttermilk
2 cups fig preserves (cut
   up large pieces of fruit)
1 cup pecans, chopped

Cream sugar with butter or margarine until light and fluffy; beat in
eggs and vanilla. Combine dry ingredients and add to creamed mixture alternately with the buttermilk; stir in fig preserves and pecans.
Spoon batter into buttered 10″ Bundt pan and bake in the middle of
preheated 350-degree oven about 1 hour or until done. Cool on rack
for 20 minutes, invert cake onto the rack and cool thoroughly. Good
as is or frost as desired.

CORONA COFFEE CAKE

*The quilting bee of yesteryear may be today's bridge-luncheon; but what-
ever the occasion — morning coffee, Sunday brunch, or PTA breakfast-
meeting — Corona Coffee cake will create sweeter relationships.*

Yield: 9 (3″) squares.

1 tsp. soda
¹/₄ tsp. salt
1 cup boiling water
1¹/₂ cups dates, pitted and
   diced
3 tbsp. butter or
   margarine

1 cup Imperial
   Granulated Sugar
1 egg, separated
1¹/₂ cups all-purpose
   flour
¹/₂ cup walnuts or pecans,
   chopped
Whipped Cream

Combine soda, salt and boiling water. Pour over dates and let stand
20 minutes. Cream butter or margarine and sugar together; beat in
egg yolk, then stir in date mixture and the flour. Stir in nuts, then
fold in egg white which has beaten until stiff but not dry. Pour batter

into a buttered 9″ square pan and bake in preheated 350-degree oven 25 to 30 minutes. Cool and cut into squares. Serve with whipped cream.

FREDERICKSBURG CHOCOLATE POTATO CAKE

Most Southwesterners will say "chocolate" instead of "vanilla." Fredericksburg Chocolate Potato Cake — moist, chocolatey and delicious — is easily a favorite.

Yield: 1 10″ Bundt cake or 1 12″ x 8″ x 2″ cake

2 cups Imperial Granulated Sugar	4 eggs, lightly beaten
1 cup shortening	2 tsp. soda
2 cups mashed potatoes (no butter or salt)	1 cup buttermilk
	¹/₂ cup cocoa
1 tsp. salt	2 cups all-purpose flour
2 tsp. cinnamon	2 cups raisins, soaked in hot water, drained
1 tsp. cloves	1 cup nuts, chopped
1 tsp. nutmeg	

Cream together the sugar, shortening, mashed potatoes and the seasonings until thoroughly combined and free from any lumps. Add eggs and beat well. Combine soda and buttermilk and let stand a few minutes. Combine cocoa and flour well and add alternately with liquid to creamed mixture. Stir in raisins and nuts. Turn batter into greased and floured 10″ Bundt pan or 12″ x 8″ x 2″ pan. Bake in preheated 350-degree oven 50 to 60 minutes, or until cake tests done.

FRONTIER PECAN CAKE

Indians enjoyed pecans long before the white man arrived in the Southwest. The Algonquins called any very hard-shelled nut a "paccan," hence pecan. This favorite pecan cake is festive enough for the holidays.

Yield: 1 (10″) tube cake

2 cups butter or
  margarine
4¹/₂ cups all-purpose
  flour
¹/₄ tsp. salt
1 tsp. baking powder
6 eggs, separated

1 carton (1 lb.) Imperial
  Brown Sugar
¹/₂ cup milk
1 tsp. vanilla
3 tbsp. strong coffee,
  optional
2 cups (8 oz.) pecans,
  chopped

Have butter or margarine at room temperature. Combine flour, salt and baking powder. Separate eggs; beat egg whites until stiff but not dry, then beat egg yolks well.

In large mixing bowl, cream together butter and brown sugar. Add beaten egg yolks, mixing well. Combine milk, vanilla and coffee. Add alternately to batter with dry ingredients. Fold in pecans and beaten egg whites. Bake in greased (bottom only) 10″ tube pan in preheated 325-degree oven for about 1 hour. Let cool in pan on rack, then remove from pan. Keeps well when securely wrapped.

Delicious as it is. Or serve with Whipped Cream Imperial: Combine 1 cup whipping cream, ¹/₈ tsp. salt, ¹/₂ tsp. vanilla and ¹/₂ cup sieved brown sugar (do not pack). Chill 1 hour. Beat with beater until stiff.

LULING WATERMELON CAKE

There was lots of work; there was little play in the early Southwest. An inventive cook, perhaps in Luling, Texas, where the watermelon reigns supreme, combined both by inventing watermelon cake.

Yield: 1 Bundt cake

1 cup shortening
3 cups Imperial
  Granulated Sugar
5 eggs (1 cupful), at room
  temperature
1 tbsp. vanilla
3 cups all-purpose flour
¹/₂ tsp. soda

¹/₂ tsp. salt
1 cup buttermilk, at room
  temperature
Red and green food color
¹/₂ cup dried currants
Imperial 10X Powdered
  Sugar Icing

Thoroughly cream shortening. Gradually add the sugar and beat with shortening until creamy. Add eggs and vanilla and beat well. Combine dry ingredients and add alternately with buttermilk, beginning and ending with flour mixture. Tint half of the batter medium pink with red food color. Tint one-fourth of batter medium green; leave one-fourth of batter white. Spread a thin layer of green batter into a greased and floured Bundt pan using two spoons, one to dip into batter and the other to scrape batter from spoon into pan. Spread a white layer of batter over the green batter. Stir currants into red batter and gently pour over the white batter. Bake in preheated 275-degree oven for 15 minutes; turn heat up to 350 degrees and bake approximately 45 minutes longer, or until cake tests done. Let cool about 10 minutes before unmolding on cake rack.

Imperial 10X Powdered Sugar Icing:

Combine 2 cups Imperial 10X Powdered Sugar, 2 tbsp. soft butter or margarine, a few drops of green food color, and 2 to 3 tbsp. of milk or enough to make proper spreading consistency. With cake on serving platter and with paper strips under edges of cake, drizzle icing over top and sides of cake in an irregular pattern. When icing has set, remove paper strips.

HOUMA HOLIDAY CAKE

Beautiful cakes are a tradition in the Southwest. Even in a dugout or a log cabin, pioneer women baked cakes for Christmas festivities and other happy times.

Yield: 1 (9″) cake

4 egg whites
¹/₂ cup Imperial
    Granulated Sugar
2 cups plus 2 tbsp. all-
    purpose flour
1 cup Imperial
    Granulated Sugar
3¹/₂ tsp. baking powder

1 tsp. salt
¹/₂ cup shortening
1 cup milk
²/₃ cup shredded or flaked
    coconut
³/₄ tsp. vanilla or almond
    flavoring

Beat egg whites until frothy; add ¹/₂ cup sugar and beat until stiff and glossy but not dry. Combine flour, 1 cup sugar, baking powder, salt and shortening; add milk and blend on low mixer speed 30 seconds, then beat 2 minutes on medium speed. Fold in egg whites, coconut, and flavoring. Pour into 2 greased and floured 9″ layer cake pans. Bake in preheated 350-degree oven 25 to 30 minutes, or until done. Cool on racks. Fill between layers and frost sides and top with Fluffy Frosting.

Fluffy Frosting:

$1^{1}/_{2}$ cups Imperial $^{1}/_{2}$ tsp. cream of tartar
    Granulated Sugar   2 tsp. vanilla
$^{1}/_{2}$ cup water   Shredded coconut
2 egg whites, unbeaten

Combine sugar and water in saucepan; cook over medium heat, stirring to dissolve sugar, until mixture comes to boil. Let boil about 30 seconds, then pour syrup over remaining ingredients in mixer bowl. Beat until frosting is stiff and holds well-defined peaks; do not under-beat. Spread on cake. Sprinkle with coconut, if desired.

INTERSTATE 45-MINUTE
CREAM CHEESE SQUARES

It's a long trip from the days of the covered wagon and mule train to interstate superhighways and supersonic flight. Interstate 45-minute Cream Cheese Cake salutes high-tech travel and state-of-the art food.

Yield: 48 (1″) squares

$^{1}/_{2}$ cup (1 stick) butter   1 cup Imperial Brown
    or margarine, melted   Sugar, packed
1 egg, beaten   1 cup Imperial 10X
1 box (about 20 oz.)   Powdered Sugar,
    yellow cake mix   unsifted
1 (8-oz.) pkg. cream   1 tsp. vanilla
    cheese, softened   Pinch of salt
2 eggs, beaten   Additional 10X Powdered
                            Sugar

Combine melted butter or margarine, egg and cake mix; spread mixture in buttered 9" x 13" pan. Combine softened cream cheese, eggs, brown sugar and powdered sugar, vanilla and salt; beat until smooth. Spread cream cheese mixture over cake mixture. Bake in preheated 325-degree oven about 45 minutes, or until cake is golden brown on top. Cut into small squares and sprinkle with powdered sugar.

CHECOTAH CHOCOLATE SHEET CAKE

In the Southwest, chili, cilantro and cumin spark up many foods; but when it comes to dessert, chocolate is still the choice in places like Checotah, Oklahoma.

Yield: 1 ($15^1/_2$" x $10^1/_2$ x 1") cake

2 cups Imperial Granulated Sugar	1 cup water
2 cups all-purpose flour	3 tbsp. cocoa
$^1/_2$ cup (1 stick) butter or margarine	$^1/_2$ cup buttermilk
$^1/_2$ cup shortening	1 tsp. soda
	1 tsp. vanilla
	2 eggs

Combine sugar and flour in large mixing bowl. Melt butter or margarine in saucepan; add shortening, water and cocoa and bring to a boil; pour over sugar-flour mixture and blend well. Add remaining ingredients and mix well to remove all lumps. Bake in greased and floured jelly roll pan ($15^1/_2$" x $10^1/_2$" x 1") in preheated 375-degree oven for 20 minutes or until cake tests done. Frost with Chocolate Frosting.

Chocolate Frosting:

$^1/_2$ cup (1 stick) butter or margarine	1 carton (1 lb.) Imperial 10X Powdered Sugar
6 tbsp. milk	1 tsp. vanilla
3 tbsp. cocoa	1 cup chopped pecans

Melt butter or margarine; add milk and cocoa and heat. Add remaining ingredients and mix well to remove lumps. Spread over hot cake.

MARBLE FALLS ANGEL FOOD CAKE

The Southwest as "new" country still carries a cowboys-and-Indians image. Marble Falls Angel Food Cake will correct that hype.

Yield: 1 (10") tube cake

1¹/₂ cups Imperial Granulated Sugar, divided	1¹/₂ cups egg whites (about 12)
1 cup cake flour, sifted	1 tsp. cream of tartar
¹/₂ tsp. salt	1 tsp. vanilla
	¹/₂ tsp. almond flavoring
	2 tbsp. cocoa

Have ingredients at room temperature and be certain that all equipment is free from grease when making angel food cakes. Combine ³/₄ cup sugar and flour; sift. Beat egg whites with the salt until foamy. Sprinkle cream of tartar over egg whites and continue to beat until stiff but not dry. Fold remaining ³/₄ cup sugar into egg whites, a few tbsp. at a time; fold in vanilla and almond flavorings. Remove about ¹/₃ of the batter to another bowl and fold the cocoa into it. Add the plain and chocolate batters alternately into an ungreased 10-inch tube pan, gently swirling with spoon to produce marbled effect. Bake in preheated 325-degree oven about one hour or until top of cake is golden. Invert pan immediately on cake rack and let cool one hour before removing cake from pan. A thin glaze of plain or chocolate powdered-sugar icing is especially welcome on this delicious cake.

MISSION MINIATURE FRUIT CAKES

Early missions, some in ruins and some restored, retain high visitor interest in parts of the Southwest. Pioneer mission folk would be dazzled by these little beauties.

Yield: 1 (8" x 4" x 3") cake and about 48 small cakes.

1¹/₂ cups white raisins,
  chopped
1¹/₂ cups candied
  pineapple, diced
1¹/₂ cups candied
  cherries, diced
1¹/₂ cups candied citron,
  chopped
2 cups pecans, chopped
¹/₂ cup red wine
³/₄ cup butter or
  margarine
1 cup Imperial Brown
  Sugar

1 tbsp. cinnamon
1¹/₂ tsp. nutmeg
¹/₂ tsp. each allspice and
  ginger
3 eggs, well beaten
2¹/₄ cups all-purpose
  flour
1 tsp. baking powder
¹/₂ tsp. salt
¹/₄ cup molasses
1 cup (10 oz.) strawberry
  preserves

Combine fruits and nuts and mix with wine. Cream butter, sugar and spices together until light and fluffy. Beat in eggs thoroughly. Combine flour, baking powder and salt and stir into the creamed mixture. Stir in molasses and preserves. Stir in fruit mixture and stir until well combined.

Spoon 5 cups batter into greased and floured 8″ x 4″ x 3″ loaf pan. Spoon remaining batter (3 cups) into greased and floured 1³/₄″ muffin tins. Bake loaf in preheated 300-degree oven about 2 hours. Bake small cakes about 45 minutes, being careful not to overbake. Cool cakes in pans 15 minutes, then turn out on wire racks to cool. If desired, ice small cakes with powdered sugar icing and sprinkle with silver or multi-colored decorations. If desired, line muffin tins with fluted paper cups.

DULCE STRAWBERRY SHORTCAKE

Dulce, New Mexico, brings new meaning to sweet, good-tasting straw-berry shortcake.

Yield: 8–10 servings

³/₄ cup shortening
1¹/₂ cups Imperial
   Granulated Sugar
3 egg yolks, beaten
2¹/₄ cups all-purpose
   flour
¹/₂ tsp. salt
3¹/₂ tsp. baking powder
³/₄ cup cold water
¹/₄ cup crushed
   strawberries

1 tsp. almond extract
3 egg whites, stiffly
   beaten
1 cup whipping cream
2 tbsp. Imperial 10X
   Powdered Sugar
2 pints fresh strawberries
¹/₂ cup Imperial 10X
   Powdered Sugar

Cream shortening and sugar; add beaten egg yolks and beat well. Add well-combined dry ingredients alternately with the water, crushed strawberries and almond extract. Fold in stiffly beaten egg whites. Bake in 2 waxed-paper-lined 9″ round cake pans in preheated 350-degree oven for about 20 minutes, or until cakes test done. Cool cakes on racks and remove from pans. Whip cream with 2 tbsp. powdered sugar; sweeten sliced strawberries with ¹/₂ cup of powdered sugar. Put cake layers together with layers of cream and berries. Top with more whipped cream and decorate with whole, perfect berries.

STRAWBERRY'S STRAWBERRY CAKE

Strawberry, Arkansas, has a special fondness for strawberry cake. This one is a dream to the tastebuds wherever you hang your cowboy hat.

Yield: 1 10″ tube cake or 1 9″ cake

1 (20-oz.) pkg. white cake
   mix
3 tbsp. all-purpose flour
3 eggs
³/₄ cup cooking oil

³/₄ cup water
1 (3-oz.) pkg. strawberry
   jello
¹/₂ cup frozen or fresh
   strawberries, sliced

Combine all ingredients in large mixer bowl and mix well. Bake in greased and floured 10″ tube pan in preheated 350-degree oven for about 40 minutes, or in two 9″ layer cake pans for about 25 minutes, or until cake tests done.

For frosting, combine 2 tbsp. melted butter or margarine, 1¹/₂ cups Imperial 10X Powdered Sugar and 2 tbsp. crushed strawberries. Drizzle over warm cake, then decorate with perfect whole strawberries and mint leaves. Display this beauty on grandma's antique crystal cake stand for extra excitement.

ROCKY ROAD CHOCOLATE CAKE

Not every road is smooth, even in the Southwest. But that's OK in Rocky, Oklahoma, if the road leads to this chocolate cake.

Yield: 1 (13″ x 9″) cake

4 eggs, beaten
1¹/₂ cups self-rising flour
1 cup butter or margarine, melted and cooled
¹/₄ cup cocoa

1¹/₄ cups Imperial Granulated Sugar
1 cup Imperial Brown Sugar
2 tsp. vanilla

Beat eggs until light; add remaining ingredients and mix until well blended. Pour into greased and floured 13″ x 9″ pan. Bake in preheated 350-degree oven for about 45 minutes, or until cake tests done. Frost in pan with Rocky Road Frosting while cake is hot.

Rocky Road Frosting:

1 6-oz. pkg. miniature marshmallows
4³/₄ cups Imperial 10X Powdered Sugar
¹/₄ cup cocoa
6 tbsp. milk

¹/₄ cup butter or margarine, melted and cooled
1 cup pecans, chopped and toasted

Arrange marshmallows over top of hot cake. Sift powdered sugar and cocoa together; blend in milk and butter or margarine. Stir in toasted nuts. Spread frosting over marshmallows and cool. Cut into squares.

NOTE: For each cup self-rising flour, substitute 1 cup all-purpose flour, 1¹/₂ tsp. baking powder and ¹/₂ tsp. salt.

ORCHARD APPLE CAKE

*Some of the best cooks in the Southwest live in small towns like Orchard,
Texas — they love this apple cake whether it's made with fresh apples
from the orchard or from the store.*

Yield: 1 (13" x 9") cake or 1 Bundt or tube cake

3 cups chopped and cored unpeeled apple	1 tsp. salt
1/2 cup raisins	1 tsp. cinnamon
1 cup pecans, chopped	2 eggs, well beaten
3 cups all-purpose flour	1 1/4 cups cooking oil
2 cups Imperial Granulated Sugar	1 1/2 tsp. vanilla
1 1/2 tsp. soda	Heavy cream, whipped for topping

Combine apples, raisins and nuts; toss together. In another bowl,
combine dry ingredients thoroughly. Beat eggs, oil and vanilla together.

Add dry ingredients to the fruit mixture and stir until well
mixed. Add egg mixture; mix well. Transfer batter to greased and
floured 13" x 9" loaf pan (or Bundt or tube pan). Bake in preheated
350-degree oven 1 to 1 1/4 hours (1 1/2 hours for Bundt or tube pan).

SUGAR LAND PARTY CAKE

*The Imperial Sugar refinery in Sugar Land, Texas, produces enough
pure cane sugar every day for every man, woman and child in the Southwest to have one of these lovely cakes. How sweet it is!*

Yield: 1 (9") cake

2/3 cup shortening	2 tsp. baking powder
2 cups Imperial Granulated Sugar	1 cup water
1 tsp. vanilla	4 egg whites, stiffly beaten
3 cups all-purpose flour	1 tsp. baking powder
1/4 tsp. salt	

Thoroughly cream shortening and sugar; stir in vanilla. Add combined flour, salt and 2 tsp. baking powder alternately with the water, beating well after each addition. Beat egg whites with 1 tsp. baking powder until stiff but not dry; fold into batter. Bake in 2 wax paper-lined 9-inch cake pans in preheated 350-degree oven about 20 minutes or until cakes test done. Put layers together with Lemon Filling and frost with Fluffy Frosting (see Holiday Cake).

Lemon Filling:

Yield: 1 cup

1/2 **cup butter or margarine**	**3 egg yolks**
1 cup Imperial Granulated Sugar	**Juice and rind, grated, of 2 lemons**

Cream butter or margarine and sugar. Add the egg yolks, grated rind and juice of the lemons. Cook over low heat, stirring constantly, until mixture comes to a boil. Simmer for 2 minutes or until filling is a clear yellow. Cool.

TRINITY RIVER MUD CAKE

The Southwestern passion for chocolate desserts goes on and on. Trinity River Mud Cake is sweetly addictive — a reputation-maker!

Yield: 1 (13" x 9" x 2") cake

4 eggs	**1/3 cup cocoa**
2 cups Imperial Granulated Sugar	**1 tsp. vanilla**
1 cup (2 sticks) butter or margarine, melted	**1 cup shredded coconut**
1 1/2 cups all-purpose flour	**2 cups (8 oz.) pecans, chopped**
	2 cups miniature marshmallows

Combine eggs and sugar in mixer and mix at high speed for 5 minutes. Combine melted butter or margarine, flour, cocoa, vanilla, coconut and nuts. Combine the two mixtures and mix well. Bake in

greased and floured 13" x 9" x 2" pan in preheated 350-degree oven
for 30 minutes or until cake tests done. Remove from oven and
spread marshmallows over cake. Frost with Floodtide Frosting while
cake is still warm.

Floodtide Frosting:

¹/₂ cup (1 stick) butter or
   margarine, melted
6 tbsp. milk
¹/₃ cup cocoa

1 pound (4 cups unsifted)
   Imperial 10X Powdered
   Sugar
1 tsp. vanilla
2 cups (8 oz.) pecans,
   chopped

Combine all frosting ingredients and mix well with wire whisk.
Spread over marshmallow-topped cake.

NOTE: Cut in small squares to enchant lots of Texas appetites.

THE SOUTHWESTERNER CAKE

*If there's anything Southwesterners like, it's getting the job done to make
time for a mid-day nap under the old cottonwood tree. This cake goes together real fast.*

Yield: 1 (10") tube pan

3 sticks (³/₄ pound) butter
   or margarine, at room
   temperature
1 carton (1 lb.) Imperial
   Brown Sugar
6 eggs, at room
   temperature

1 carton (1 lb.) Imperial
   all-purpose flour
1 tsp. lemon juice
1 tbsp. vanilla

Cream butter or margarine; add brown sugar and beat until fluffy.
Add eggs, one at a time, beating well after each addition.
    Gradually add flour to batter. Add lemon juice and vanilla and
mix well. Bake in greased and floured 10" tube pan in preheated
325-degree oven approximately 1 hour. Cool 4 minutes, then invert

pan. Serve plain, with whipped cream, with fruit or ice cream. If desired, sprinkle cooled cake with sifted Imperial 10X Powdered Sugar. To make GOLDEN WESTERNER CAKE, use one (1 lb.) carton of Imperial 10X Powdered Sugar instead of Imperial Brown Sugar.

Candies

OKAY CANDIED PEANUTS

1893 Oklahoma land rushers would be amazed at the difference one hundred years can make. The grasslands now produce oil wells and crops such as top quality peanuts to make this crunchy, nutty confection.

Yield: about 3 cups

2 cups raw peanuts	**¹/₂ cup water**
1 cup Imperial	**Salt**
Granulated Sugar	

In heavy saucepan, combine peanuts, sugar and water. Over medium-low heat, cook while stirring until mixture crystallizes and coats peanuts, about 10 minutes. Sprinkle with a little salt. Store in covered container.

CHICO-CHOCO CONFECTIONS

Southwesterners are energetic, fast-moving, think-ahead folks. You can bet your bottom dollar Chico, Texas, will be ready with delicious munchies when Southwest Conference games roll around.

Yield: about 5 dozen

1 6-oz. pkg. chocolate
   morsels
1/3 cup strong hot coffee
3 tbsp. light corn syrup
3 cups Imperial 10X
   Powdered Sugar, sifted

1 cup chopped nuts
1¼ cups vanilla wafer
   crumbs
1 cup flaked or shredded
   coconut

Melt chocolate morsels over very low heat until partially melted; remove from heat and stir until smooth. Blend in hot coffee, corn syrup and powdered sugar. Add nuts, crumbs and ½ cup of the coconut. Shape mixture into 1-inch balls and roll each in the remaining coconut. Store in tightly covered container 2 days for best flavor.

DELTA DATE LOAF

Southwestern pecan groves supply top quality pecans October through December. Refrigerate shelled nuts up to three months; store frozen for two years. You'll be all set to make delicious snackies like Delta Date Loaf.

Yield: 1 loaf

1½ cups Imperial
   Granulated Sugar
1½ cups Imperial Brown
   Sugar
1 cup milk
1 cup dates, pitted and
   chopped

1 cup pecans, chopped
1 tbsp. butter or
   margarine
1 tsp. vanilla

In heavy saucepan, combine both sugars and the milk; cook over medium heat to the soft ball stage, 234 degrees F. on a candy thermometer. Add dates, pecans and butter or margarine and continue to cook, stirring occasionally, to firm ball stage or 248 degrees F. on candy thermometer. Add vanilla and let cool. Beat till creamy and stiff. Empty onto a damp towel or cloth; shape into loaf. Wrap with towel, then with foil or plastic wrap. Store until ready to serve, then slice in ¼-inch slices with a sharp knife.

DEVINE DIVINITY

There are several climate zones in the huge Southwest. In humid areas, choose candymaking days with care. In arid zones, such as Devine, Texas, make Devine Divinity just about any time.

Yield: about 1¹/₂ pounds.

2¹/₂ cups Imperial
   Granulated Sugar
¹/₂ cup white corn syrup
¹/₂ cup water
2 egg whites, stiffly
   beaten

1 tsp. vanilla
¹/₂ cup slivered gum drop
   candies or 1 cup
   chopped walnuts

Combine sugar, syrup and water in saucepan over low heat, stirring until sugar dissolves. Cook until candy thermometer registers 260 degrees F. Remove from heat and cool slightly. Beat egg whites until stiff; pour hot mixture very slowly over egg whites, beating constantly. Continue beating until candy becomes very stiff and loses its glossy appearance. Beat a few strokes by hand to improve texture. Add vanilla and drop by large spoonfuls onto waxed paper. Push slivered gum drops or walnuts into the candy.

AVERY ISLAND BARBECUED PECANS

Southwesterners are a hard-working bunch. They're smart, too, and break for happy times with family and friends. Avery Island Barbecued Pecans make relaxing more fun.

Yield: 2 cups

1 tbsp. Imperial
   Granulated Sugar
2 tbsp. cider vinegar or
   white vinegar
2 cups pecan halves

1 tsp. butter or margarine
¹/₂ tsp. salt or seasoned
   salt
1 drop hot pepper sauce
   (or to your taste)

Combine sugar and vinegar in a quart jar; add pecans and shake vigorously to coat nuts. Transfer nuts to a shallow baking pan and toast in preheated 250-degree oven, stirring frequently, until lightly browned. Add butter or margarine, salt and hot pepper sauce; toss to coat nuts. Continue baking until toasted, being careful pecans don't burn. Cool and store in airtight container. Refrigeration keeps them crisp but bring to room temperature before serving.

DESERT RAINBOW JELLY MINTS

Capture the brilliant hues of the Southwest inside these jelly-filled mints for parties and other good times.

Yield: about 6 dozen pieces

1 carton (1 lb.) Imperial $^1/_8$ tsp. salt
   10X Powdered Sugar $^1/_4$ cup water
$^1/_4$ tsp. peppermint   Gumdrops cut into
   extract   narrow strips

Combine powdered sugar, peppermint extract and salt in mixing bowl; add water gradually, stirring until sugar is completely moistened. Knead until mixture is stiff enough to roll out. Divide candy into small portions, about $1^1/_2$ tbsp. each. Flatten each portion into a rectanguler shape and place several strips of gum drops in center; roll candy around them. Slice.

INDIANOLA CARAMEL CORN

Indianola Caramel Corn evokes the fun and drama of the circus tent. Make it by the gallon for parties, TV evenings and for gifts, whether or not Indianola, Oklahoma, is your hometown.

Yield: about 5 quarts (2 pounds)

1 cup popcorn kernels (to
  yield 5 qts. popped
  corn)
1 cup (2 sticks) butter or
  margarine
2 cups Imperial Brown
  Sugar, firmly packed

¹/₂ cup light corn syrup
1 tsp. salt
¹/₂ tsp. soda
2 cups toasted nuts,
  optional

Pop corn and keep warm in large roasting pan in oven. Combine remaining ingredients, except soda and nuts, in 2-quart heavy saucepan over medium heat. Stir until brown sugar dissolves, then continue to boil to firm ball stage, 248 degrees F. on candy
thermometer. Remove from heat and stir in soda. Pour hot syrup
over popped corn and nuts, stirring to combine well. Return to preheated 250-degree oven for 15 minutes; stir corn and repeat heating
and stirring 2 more times. Cool thoroughly and store in airtight containers in cool place. Makes great gift packages.

BAYOU COUNTRY CHOCOLATE MORSELS

*Louisiana folks love good food, from seafood to sweets. Which Cajun
kitchen invented these meltingly good morsels?*

Yield: about 80 pieces

2 lbs. Imperial 10X
  Powdered Sugar
1 stick (¹/₂ cup) butter
  or margarine, melted
1 can sweetened
  condensed milk

1 7-oz. can shredded
  coconut
2 cups pecans, chopped
3 6-oz. bags chocolate
  morsels
³/₄ bar paraffin

Combine all ingredients, except chocolate morsels and paraffin, in
large bowl and roll into small balls; chill. Melt chocolate and paraffin in double boiler over hot water. Dip candy morsels in chocolate-
paraffin mixture and cool on waxed paper.

PORTALES PEANUT BRITTLE

Everybody's mom deserves credit. Mine was one of the best cooks, famous for this peanut brittle made ONLY with Portales (New Mexico) peanuts.

Yield: about 2 pounds

2 cups Imperial Granulated Sugar	**2 cups raw shelled peanuts**
1/4 tsp. cream of tartar	**1/2 tsp. salt**
1 cup boiling water	**2 tbsp. butter or margarine**
1 cup white corn syrup	**1/4 tsp. baking soda**

Off heat, stir sugar and cream of tartar in boiling water until sugar is dissolved. Stir in corn syrup, peanuts and salt. Cook, stirring occasionally, to 295 degrees F. on candy thermometer. Remove from heat and barely stir in butter or margarine and soda; overstirring will counteract the build-up of bubbles that makes the candy crunchy. Pour onto a well-buttered marble slab or large cookie sheet, scraping candy from the pan. Spread the mixture rapidly with a spatula. When cool, break into chunks. Store in a tightly covered tin.

BONITA CANDY ROLL

Bonita Candy Roll is a confection that makes the candy platter so pretty — just the sort of dessert you'd expect from a town like Bonita, Louisiana.

Yield: 48 slices

2 squares unsweetened chocolate	**1 cup pecans, chopped**
2 squares semi-sweet chocolate	**1 egg, beaten**
1 tsp. butter or margarine	**1 1/2 cups multi-colored miniature marsh-mallows**
1 cup sifted Imperial 10X Powdered Sugar	

Combine both types of chocolate and the butter or margarine and melt over low heat; reserve. Combine remaining ingredients, then combine the two mixtures. Divide into four portions and shape each into a roll on coconut-lined waxed paper and wrap each candy roll in the waxed paper; chill overnight. Slice into a total of 48 slices. Store in refrigerator.

NOTE: When using egg in an uncooked dish, never use a previously cracked egg and always store finished product in refrigerator.

PANHANDLE SKILLET FUDGE

Make Panhandle Skillet Fudge in an electric skillet, and give it the creamy flavor of peanut butter. Five minutes of cooking makes it. Yummy!

Yield: 16 (2") squares.

2 cups Imperial Granulated Sugar	1 cup miniature marshmallows
3 tbsp. butter or margarine	1 12-oz. jar chunk style peanut butter
1 cup evaporated milk	1 tsp. vanilla

Combine sugar, butter or margarine and milk in large electric skillet with dial set at 280 degrees F. Bring to boil and boil 5 minutes, stirring constantly. Turn off heat and add marshmallows, peanut butter and vanilla. Stir until all is melted and blended. Turn into buttered 8" pan and cool well before cutting into squares.

BOURBON STREET PRALINES

Only in New Orleans can you get pralines as good as these, except in your own kitchen. They're easier to make than falling off a log backwards, as any Southwestern kid would say!

Yield: about 1 pound

3 cups Imperial Brown Sugar	1–2 tbsp. butter
1/4 tsp. salt	1 tsp. vanilla
1 cup milk or cream	1 cup pecans, halves or coarsely chopped

Combine brown sugar, salt and milk or cream in heavy saucepan; cover and cook about 3 minutes until steam washes down any sugar crystals from sides of pan. Uncover and cook slowly, without stirring, to 238 degrees F. Remove candy from heat, add the butter and cool to 110 degrees F. without stirring. After cooling, beat until smooth and creamy. Add the vanilla and nuts. Drop candy from a spoon onto a buttered surface. If candy hardens before it is all out of the pan, set pan in hot water.

FORT BLISS CANDIED WALNUTS

No matter which Southwestern state you call home, you'll find these confections blissfully easy to make and easier to eat.

Yield: about 3 cups

1 cup Imperial Granulated Sugar	1 tsp. vanilla
5 tsp. water	2 cups English walnut (or Texas pecan) halves
1 tsp. cinnamon	

Combine the first four ingredients; bring to boil. Remove from heat and stir in nuts. Continue to stir for a few minutes, then lift nuts from syrup with fork, separate them and allow to dry on rack over waxed paper.

TEXOMA TOFFEE

Texas and Oklahoma fans may disagree on football teams, but one thing they agree on is good food. Texoma Toffee was designed to satisfy the sweet tooth of everyone — not just Southwesterners.

Yield: 1 pound

1 **cup butter or margarine**
1 **cup Imperial**
   Granulated Sugar
1 **6-oz. pkg. chocolate**
   morsels

¹/₂ **cup finely minced nuts**
   such as blanched
   almonds

Butter a 9-inch square pan generously; reserve. Combine butter or margarine and the sugar in a small heavy saucepan. Cook over moderate heat, stirring constantly, until thermometer registers 310 degrees F.; candy should be caramel color and a small amount of syrup should be brittle when immersed in water. Pour candy quickly into buttered pan; let cool to harden. Melt chocolate morsels in top of double boiler over hot water; spread half of melted chocolate over surface of hardened candy. Let cool until chocolate is also hardened. Using a pancake turner, turn candy over and spread remaining melted chocolate over second side. Sprinkle minced nuts over chocolate and gently press them into the chocolate. Let cool again until chocolate is hardened. Break into pieces. To develop flavor, store in a tightly covered tin for at least 2 days.

TEXARKANA CHOCOLATE TRUFFLES

Texas and Arkansas fans agree! They all like Texarkana Chocolate Truffles. Problem is these goodies are so quick to disappear.

Yield: about 1 pound

4 **squares unsweetened**
   chocolate
¹/₂ **cup butter**
2 **cups sifted Imperial**
   10X Powdered Sugar

4 **egg yolks**
1 **tsp. vanilla**
Cocoa or ground
   toasted nuts

Melt chocolate and butter in a small heavy saucepan over very low heat, stirring constantly. Cool. Stir in sugar until smooth. Beat in egg yolks, 1 at a time. Beat in vanilla. Chill until mixture is firm enough to shape. Using 2 teaspoons, scoop a rounded teaspoonful of mixture and push off with the other spoon into cocoa or nuts. Roll in coating to form perfect balls. Place in a shallow pan and chill until firm. Store covered in refrigerator.

NOTE: Whenever using egg in an uncooked finished product, never use a cracked egg, and keep finished product refrigerated.

WALNUT RIDGE WALNUT FUDGE

You'll say something clever like "Magnifique!" when you taste Walnut Ridge Fudge. Folks in Walnut Ridge, Arkansas, always ask for "More!"

Yield: 1 pound

1 4-oz. pkg. regular
  vanilla pudding mix
2 tbsp. butter or
  margarine
1/4 cup milk

1³/4 cups Imperial 10X
  Powdered Sugar,
  sifted
1/4 tsp. black walnut or
  vanilla flavoring
1/2 cup walnuts, chopped

Combine pudding mix, butter or margarine and milk in saucepan and bring to boil over medium heat. Boil 1 minute, stirring constantly. Remove from heat and stir in powdered sugar and flavoring, blending well. Stir in nuts and pour into greased 8″ x 4″ pan. Cool and cut into squares or bars.

Cookies

CHOCOLATE CHIPPERS

New Mexico potatoes are trucked to North Texas where they're made into potato chips which are then delivered all over the Southwest. Some of these chips turn up in Chocolate Chippers.

Yield: 8 dozen cookies.

1 **pound (4 sticks) butter
   or margarine**
3¹/₂ **cups all-purpose
   flour**
1 **cup Imperial
   Granulated Sugar**

2 **tsp. vanilla**
2 **cups crushed potato
   chips**
2 **cups crushed corn
   flakes**
1 **cup chocolate morsels**

Combine and mix well the butter or margarine, flour, sugar and vanilla. Stir in the potato chips, corn flakes and chocolate morsels. Drop by teaspoonfuls onto ungreased cookie sheet. Bake in preheated 375-degree oven for 10 to 12 minutes.

STAINED GLASS COOKIES

Stained Glass Cookies are an idea stolen from places like St. Louis Cathedral in New Orleans.

Yield: 1 "window"

4¹/₂ **cups all-purpose
   flour**
¹/₂ **tsp. salt**
1 **tsp. soda**
1 **cup shortening**
1¹/₂ **cups Imperial
   Granulated Sugar**

1 **tsp. vanilla**
¹/₂ **tsp. almond extract**
¹/₃ **cup (about 2 large)
   eggs**
Stained Glass Icing

Combine dry ingredients. Cream together the shortening, sugar, vanilla, almond extract and the eggs; combine the two mixtures. Chill dough thoroughly. With dough on a flat baking sheet lined with greased brown paper or baker's parchment, roll dough to 1/8" thickness. Using a table knife, cut dough into free-form shaped cookies to resemble a stained glass window, being sure there is space between pieces so they won't bake together. Bake cookies in preheated 350-degree oven about 8 minutes or until lightly browned. Remove cookies to rack to cool keeping them in the same order as they were on the baking sheet. Frost with Stained Glass Icing.

Stained Glass Icing

1 1-pound box Imperial
   10X Powdered Sugar
3 tbsp. butter or
   margarine, softened
1 tsp. vanilla

¹/₄ cup milk or light
     cream
Artificial food colors of
   your choice

Combine all ingredients and blend well, adjusting sugar and cream for correct spreading consistency. Divide into several portions and tint each to achieve the design you have planned for your "stained glass window."

SORORITY SWEETHEART COOKIES

Whether you're partial to Sigma Chi or Kappa Delta, these cookies are just right for a Southwest Conference sweetheart.

Yield: 40 cookies

1³/₄ cups Imperial
      Granulated Sugar
³/₄ pound (3 sticks)
     unsalted butter
2 eggs, beaten lightly
3 cups all-purpose flour

1¹/₂ cups cocoa
¹/₄ tsp. salt
¹/₃ tsp. freshly ground
     black pepper
1 tsp. ground cinnamon
Mocha Icing

Cream sugar and butter until light and fluffy; add eggs and beat well. Combine dry ingredients, stirring by hand into the butter mixture until thoroughly mixed. More flour may be necessary if dough is too soft. Divide dough into three portions, wrap each in plastic wrap and chill for at least 1 hour.

On a well-floured board, roll out the chilled dough to ¹/₈ inch thick; cut into 3-inch hearts and place them on buttered wax paper-lined or baker's-parchment-lined baking sheet. Bake in preheated 375-degree oven about 8 minutes, or until done. Cool on wire racks. Make Mocha Icing and spread on cooled cookies.

Mocha Icing

1 cup Imperial 10X
   Powdered Sugar, sifted
1 tbsp. coffee (regular or
   instant)

1 tsp. cocoa
2 tbsp. pecans, ground,
   optional

Combine all icing ingredients and mix thoroughly, adjusting for spreading consistency. Spread over cookies, cool on racks and store in airtight containers.

DIANA CHRISTMAS SUGAR COOKIES

Lots of Southwestern Dianas can claim this delicious cookie, but there is only one Diana, Texas.

Yield: about 4 dozen

2 cups all-purpose flour
1 tsp. baking powder
$^1/_2$ tsp. salt
$^1/_2$ cup shortening

1 cup Imperial
   Granulated Sugar
1 egg
$^1/_4$ cup milk
$^1/_2$ tsp. lemon extract

Combine flour, baking powder and salt; set aside. Blend shortening and sugar; mix in the egg. Add dry ingredients alternately with milk and lemon extract; blend thoroughly. Chill dough overnight for best results. When ready to bake, roll dough to $^1/_4''$ thickness on floured surface. Cut out cookie shapes with knife or cookie cutters. Use round cutters for plain cookies and fancy cutters for other seasons as desired. Transfer cookies to greased cookie sheet and bake in preheated 400-degree oven 7 to 10 minutes or until done.

Decorating and Icing

$3^3/_4$ cups Imperial 10X
   Powdered Sugar
   (1-lb.carton)

$^1/_4$ cup milk
   (approximate)
Food colorings and
   decorations as desired

Combine powdered sugar and milk; stir until smooth. Add more milk, 1 tsp. at a time, to achieve desired spreading consistency. Divide icing into several small bowls and tint with several drops of food coloring. Trim with colored decorator sprinkles, cinnamon red hots and other candies.

BAYLOR BARS

Baylor Bars are a variation of pecan pie but easier to make and easier to serve. They're perfect for after-the-game feasting.

Yield: about 24 squares

Crust:

2 cups all-purpose flour   1 cup (2 sticks) butter or
$^1/_4$ tsp. salt   margarine
$^1/_4$ cup Imperial   2 tbsp. white vinegar
    Granulated Sugar

Combine dry ingredients and work in butter with fingers or pastry blender. Mix in vinegar and spread dough on bottom and up sides of 15" x 10" x 1" pan.

Filling:

$1^1/_2$ cups Imperial Brown   2 eggs, beaten
    Sugar, firmly packed $^3/_4$ cup heavy cream or
$^1/_2$ cup Imperial   evaporated milk
    Granulated Sugar $^1/_2$ tsp. vanilla
2 tbsp. all-purpose flour $^1/_2$ cup pecans, coarsely
$^1/_2$ tsp. salt   chopped

Combine all ingredients, except pecans; stir well. Stir in pecans and pour into crust. Bake in preheated 350-degree oven for 30 to 35 minutes, or until filling is set and top is caramel colored. Cool completely before cutting into 2" squares. Delicious with vanilla ice cream or whipped cream lightly sweetened with Imperial 10X Powdered Sugar and flavored with vanilla.

APPLETON OATMEAL APPLE COOKIES

A combination of fruit for good taste and good keeping quality, nuts for crunch and flavor, and oatmeal for fiber add up to a winning combination from Appleton, Arkansas.

Yield: About 120 cookies

2 cups Imperial Brown
   Sugar
1 cup butter or margarine
4 eggs, well beaten
3 cups raisins, chopped,
   or currants
2 cups apple, unpeeled
   and chopped

1 cup oats, uncooked
3¹/₂ cups all-purpose
   flour
¹/₂ tsp. salt
1 tsp. baking powder
1 tsp. soda
1 tsp. cinnamon
2 cups pecans, chopped

Thoroughly cream brown sugar and butter or margarine; add eggs and beat well. Add currants or raisins, apples and oats. Add nuts to dry ingredients and combine with first mixture. Chill overnight. Dough can be kept in refrigerator for several days and baked as needed. Drop cookies by teaspoonfuls onto greased cookie sheet. Bake in preheated 375-degree oven about 10 minutes or until cookies begin to brown around edges. These cookies freeze well.

BAR NONE LEMON BARS

The Southwest roams over mountains, plains and valleys, producing everything from wheat to citrus fruit such as lemons in the Rio Grande Valley.

Yield: 3 dozen

¹/₂ cup Imperial 10X
   Powdered Sugar
1 cup (2 sticks) butter,
   softened
2 cups all-purpose flour
¹/₄ tsp. salt

4 eggs, beaten
2 cups Imperial
   Granulated Sugar
¹/₄ cup all-purpose flour
1 tsp. lemon rind, grated
4 tsp. lemon juice

Thoroughly blend powdered sugar, butter, 2 cups flour, and salt; press into bottom of buttered 13″ x 9″ pan. Bake in preheated 350-degree oven for 20 minutes. Combine and blend remaining ingredients; pour over first layer and continue baking for 25 minutes. Sift additional powdered sugar over the top immediately after removing from oven. Cool; cut into squares.

COUGAR COOKIES

If you're a Cougar fan, you will rate these cookies A + for school spirit. Bright red jelly decorates these white cookies that will liven up any school party. Just don't feed them to the kitty!

Yield: about 2 dozen

¹/₄ **cup Imperial Brown Sugar**	1 **egg yolk**
¹/₂ **cup butter or margarine, softened**	1 **tsp. vanilla**
	1 **cup all-purpose flour**
	2 **tbsp. red jelly**

Combine brown sugar, butter or margarine, egg yolk and vanilla; beat until smooth. Blend flour into first mixture. Chill, covered, 30 minutes. Shape into 1″ balls and place them 1″ apart on ungreased cookie sheets. Bake in preheated 375-degree oven 10 to 12 minutes or until cookies are a delicate brown. Remove to wire rack; while still soft, press center of each cookie with spoon and place ¹/₄ tsp. jelly in depression of each cookie.

SAND SPRING COOKIES

Sand Spring Cookies are melt-in-the-mouth morsels — so good they're welcome on party tables and in family cookie jars from Sand Springs, Texas, to Sand Springs, Oklahoma.

Yield: 3 dozen

¹/₂ cup butter, softened
2 tbsp. Imperial
   Granulated Sugar
¹/₂ tsp. vanilla
¹/₂ cup pecans, finely
   chopped

1 cup all-purpose flour
Imperial 10X Powdered
   Sugar
Red hot cinnamon candies

Cream together butter and sugar; stir in vanilla. Combine nuts with flour and add to first mixture. Shape dough into small balls. Press several red hot candies into each ball of dough and place them 1″ apart on ungreased baking sheets and bake in preheated 375-degree oven about 10 minutes or until golden tan. Cool a few minutes, then roll in powdered sugar. Cool on racks.

RUNNING INDIAN COOKIES

These delicious cookies supply quick energy for the runners and joggers among us.

Yield: 7 dozen cookies

2 cups Imperial Brown
   Sugar
2 cups Imperial
   Granulated Sugar
³/₄ cup butter or
   margarine, softened
1 cup shortening
4 eggs, beaten
2 tsp. vanilla

3 cups all-purpose flour
2 tsp. salt
2 tsp. soda
3 cups uncooked oats
2 cups coconut
2 cups raisins
1 cup chocolate chips
1 cup pecans, chopped

Cream brown sugar, granulated sugar, butter or margarine and shortening; beat in the eggs and vanilla. Combine flour, salt, and soda and beat into first mixture. Add remaining ingredients and knead into mixture. Drop by heaping teaspoons, 2″ apart, onto greased baking sheet. Bake in preheated 350-degree oven about 8 minutes or until cookies are nicely browned. Cool on baking sheet about 1 minute before removing them to a rack to cool. Store in air-tight container. For best results, shape dough into rolls, wrap and chill several hours; then slice and bake as directed above.

OATMEAL ROLY-POLIES

Oatmeal has found a permanent home in the Southwest whether in cereal bowls, on the Texas map (there's an Oatmeal, Texas), or in delectable Oatmeal Roly-Polies.

Yield: about 48 (1″) bites

2 cups Imperial Granulated Sugar	2¹/₂ cups pecans, finely chopped (divided)
¹/₂ cup (1 stick) butter or margarine	¹/₂ cup coconut
¹/₂ cup milk	Chocolate Topping (see below)
1 tsp. vanilla	
3 cups old fashioned oats, uncooked	

Combine sugar, butter or margarine and milk in saucepan. Bring to boil and let boil for 1¹/₂ minutes. Remove from heat and stir in vanilla. Combine oats, 1 cup of the pecans and the coconut; combine the two mixtures, mixing well. Let mixture cool enough to handle and roll into 1″ balls. Let stand about one hour, then dip one side of each roly-poly into chocolate topping, then into remaining chopped pecans.

Chocolate Topping:

1 (12-oz.) pkg. semi-sweet chocolate morsels	4 tsp. butter or margarine

Melt chocolate and butter or margarine in top of double boiler, stirring to mix.

STAR CITY STAR COOKIES

Star City Star Cookies take center stage in Star City, Arkansas. They're a perky blend of spices, molasses, brown sugar and show biz.

Yield: about 4 dozen (3¹/₂″) cookies

2½ cups all-purpose
   flour
1 tsp. soda, sifted
1 tsp. cinnamon
1 tsp. ground ginger
¼ tsp. ground cloves
½ tsp. ground black
   pepper

½ cup (1 stick) unsalted
   butter cut in chunks
½ cup Imperial Brown
   Sugar
½ cup molasses
2 tsp. vinegar, preferably
   cider vinegar
1 egg yolk

Combine dry ingredients; reserve. Melt butter and add brown sugar, molasses and vinegar, stirring until sugar dissolves. Stir into the flour mixture; stir in beaten egg yolk and stir until well blended (dough will be sticky). Chill overnight, well-wrapped.

Divide dough into two portions and chill one while using the other. Roll out dough on lightly floured surface to ⅛-inch thickness. Cut out star-shaped cookies dipping cutter into flour frequently. Transfer cookies carefully to baking sheet and bake in preheated 350-degree oven 7 to 8 minutes. Cookie edges will darken, but do not overbake.

Nutmeg Icing:

1 cup Imperial 10X
   Powdered Sugar, sifted
2½ tbsp. milk

¼ tsp. ground or freshly
   grated nutmeg

Combine all ingredients and stir until smooth. Drizzle icing over cooled cookies and cool on racks until icing is set.

NOTE: Cookies will be easier to remove from baking sheets if sheets have been lined with baker's parchment (available in kitchen specialty shops).

PADRE ISLAND SAND DOLLARS

Padre Island Sand Dollars are shaped like the little sea creatures. These cookies are not for conversation only — they're good eating!

Yield: 3½ dozen cookies

1 cup (2 sticks) butter or
   margarine
¹/₂ cup Imperial 10X
   Powdered Sugar

2 cups all-purpose flour
¹/₄ tsp. salt
1 tsp. vanilla
   Imperial Granulated
   Sugar

Cream butter and powdered sugar until very fluffy. Gradually stir in flour and salt, then stir in vanilla. Shape level tbsp. of dough into balls. Press one side of each ball into the granulated sugar and place them on baking sheet with sugar side up. Cookies do not spread much so can be placed closer together than other types of cookies. Slash cookies in a few places around edges to look like marine sand dollars. Bake in preheated 400-degree oven about 10 minutes or until done but not browned. Remove from cookie sheets and cool on wire racks.

CRANFILLS GAP CRANBERRY BARS

Freeze a supply of cranberries in the plastic bags they're packed in for year-round goodies.

Yield: about 48 bars

¹/₂ cup Imperial
   Granulated Sugar
¹/₂ cup butter or
   margarine
3 egg yolks
2 cups all-purpose flour
¹/₄ tsp. salt
¹/₂ tsp. baking powder
¹/₄ cup water

1 tsp. vanilla
1¹/₃ cups canned
   cranberry-orange
   relish
3 egg whites
¹/₄ tsp. salt
¹/₂ cup Imperial
   Granulated Sugar
1 cup pecans, chopped

Beat ¹/₂ cup sugar into butter or margarine gradually; beat in the egg yolks, one at a time. Combine flour, salt and baking powder and add to creamed mixture alternately with water and vanilla. Spread in 9″ x 12″ ungreased pan. Spread cranberry-orange relish over batter. To make meringue topping, beat egg whites and salt until stiff but not dry. Gradually beat in remaining sugar until peaks are stiff.

Fold in chopped pecans. Spread meringue over the relish. Bake in preheated 350-degree oven 20 to 25 minutes. When thoroughly cool, cut into squares.

PAUL'S VALLEY GINGERSNAPS

Paul's Valley, Oklahoma, inspired these larger-than-life ginger-flavored cookies.

Yield: 18 large cookies

2 cups all-purpose flour	**$^1/_2$ cup Imperial**
1 tbsp. baking soda	**Granulated Sugar**
1 tsp. salt	**$^1/_2$ cup Imperial Brown**
$^3/_4$ tsp. each ginger,	**Sugar, packed**
cinnamon and cloves	**1 egg**
$^3/_4$ cup shortening (half	**$^1/_4$ cup molasses**
butter or margarine)	**2 cups walnuts, chopped**
	Additional Imperial
	Granulated Sugar

Combine flour with soda, salt and spices. Cream shortening, butter or margarine, granulated sugar, brown sugar and egg. Stir in molasses, then the flour mixture. Add walnuts and mix well. Shape into 1$^1/_2$″ balls and roll in additional granulated sugar. Place on greased cookie sheets and flatten to about 3$^1/_2$ inches in diameter. Bake in preheated 350-degree oven about 10 minutes. Let cool one minute before removing from baking sheet. Cool on wire rack. Store in airtight container.

NASA PEANUT BUTTER COOKIES

Space industry people, just like all the rest of us, love a good cookie. These peanut butter cookies are also spicy.

Yield: 4 dozen cookies

$^1/_2$ cup Imperial Brown
   Sugar
$^1/_2$ cup Imperial
   Granulated Sugar
$^1/_2$ cup butter or
   margarine at room
   temperature
1 egg, beaten

1 cup chunky peanut
   butter
$^1/_2$ tsp. salt
$^1/_2$ tsp. soda
$^1/_4$ tsp. cloves
$^1/_4$ tsp. ginger
$^1/_4$ tsp. cinnamon
$1^1/_2$ cups all-purpose
   flour

Cream together the brown sugar, granulated sugar and the butter or margarine. Add beaten egg, peanut butter and combined dry ingredients. Mix well and roll dough into 1″ balls. Place them on greased cookie sheets and flatten with tines of fork. Bake in preheated 375-degree oven 12 to 15 minutes.

WHITE CASTLE CHOCOLATE COOKIES

A specialty cookie for any collection of favorite cookies from White Castle, Louisiana, to Whitehall, Arkansas.

Yield: 4 dozen cookies

$^3/_4$ cup Imperial
   Granulated Sugar
$^1/_2$ cup (1 stick) butter or
   margarine
1 8-oz. bar cream cheese
   at room temperature
2 tsp. vanilla

$1^1/_2$ cups all-purpose
   flour
2 tsp. baking powder
$^3/_4$ cup walnuts, coarsely
   chopped
3 oz. white chocolate or
   white almond bark,
   broken in chunks

Cream the sugar, butter or margarine, cream cheese and the vanilla until creamy and well combined. Combine flour and baking powder and stir into creamed mixture. Stir in nuts and white chocolate or white almond bark. Drop by spoonfuls 2 inches apart onto greased baking sheets. Flatten slightly with the back of a spoon. Bake in preheated 400-degree oven for 8 to 10 minutes.

CHECKMATE CHESS SQUARES

The bar cookie is everybody's favorite. It's easy to make a large batch of these hearty sweets with a minimum of fuss — dear to the heart of any busy cook.

Yield: about 30 squares

1 1-lb. box Imperial Brown Sugar	2 tsp. baking powder
1 cup Imperial Granulated Sugar	$^1/_4$ tsp. salt
2 sticks butter or margarine, melted	1 cup pecans, chopped
4 egg yolks	$1^1/_2$ tsp. vanilla
2 cups all-purpose flour	4 egg whites
	Imperial 10X Powdered Sugar

Cream together the brown sugar, granulated sugar and the butter or margarine; beat in the egg yolks. Combine flour, baking powder and salt and add to creamed mixture. Add nuts and vanilla. Beat egg whites until stiff but not dry; fold into batter which will be quite thick. Spread batter into greased 9″ x 13″ pan and bake in preheated 350-degree oven for about 40 minutes or until done. Let cool on rack and sprinkle with powdered sugar.

Miscellaneous Desserts

ANGELIC ICEBOX TORTE

Meringue transforms desserts into angelic delights. Angelic Icebox Torte is at home in San Angelo.

Yield: about 10 servings

3 egg whites
³/₄ cup Imperial
    Granulated Sugar
³/₄ cup chocolate wafer
    crumbs
1 cup chopped nuts

1 tsp. vanilla
1 cup heavy cream,
    whipped and sweetened
1 tsp. vanilla
1 tsp. instant coffee
    powder

Beat egg whites until stiff; add sugar gradually, beating until stiff
and glossy. Fold in crumbs, nuts, and vanilla. Divide evenly into 2
well-greased 9″ cake pans and bake in preheated 350-degree oven 20
minutes. Remove from oven; when completely cool, remove one
layer to serving plate. Top with stiffly beaten cream, flavored to
taste with 1 tsp. each of vanilla and instant coffee. Add second cake
layer. Garnish with more whipped mocha cream. Chill thoroughly.

ARKANSAS FRESH APPLE KUCHEN

*Once upon a time, good fresh apples were available only in the fall and
winter. Improved varieties and distribution provide good apples year-
round. Often, they are from Arkansas orchards.*

Yield: 6–8 servings

2 cups all-purpose flour
³/₄ cup Imperial
    Granulated Sugar
¹/₂ tsp. salt
¹/₄ tsp. baking powder
¹/₂ cup butter or
    margarine

1 pound tart, cooking
    apples
¹/₂ tsp. cinnamon
¹/₄ tsp. nutmeg
2 egg yolks, beaten
1 cup heavy cream or
    evaporated (not
    condensed) milk

Combine flour, 2 tbsp. of the sugar, salt and baking powder and cut
in the butter or margarine to make coarse crumbs. Transfer to 9″
round layer cake pan or springform pan and pat firmly against bottom and 2 inches up sides of pan. Cut washed, pared and cored apples into ¹/₂-inch wedges and toss with remaining sugar and the
spices; arrange in pastry shell. Bake in preheated 400-degree oven 15
minutes; reduce heat to 350 degrees. Pour beaten egg yolks mixed

with the cream or milk over the apples and bake 30 minutes longer, or until top is golden brown. Cool on wire rack 10 minutes. Remove sides from springform pan, if used, and cut in wedges. Delicious served warm.

LE BON TEMPS RICE PUDDING

Southwesterners love a party or a festival, so we have all kinds of harvest celebrations, shrimp boat blessings, Wurstfests, and rice festivals. Festivities feature good times and good eating — like Le Bon Temps Rice Pudding.*

Yield: 4–6 servings

$^1/_2$ **cup long grain rice**	**3 eggs, beaten**
$^1/_2$ **tsp. salt**	$^1/_2$ **cup Imperial**
1 cup water	**Granulated Sugar**
1 quart milk	**1 cup raisins (white**
$^1/_2$ **stick butter or**	**raisins are best)**
margarine	$^1/_2$ **tsp. vanilla**

Add rice and salt to boiling water in a large saucepan. Cover and cook over low heat 7 to 10 minutes, or until water is absorbed. Add milk and butter or margarine, stir and bring to boil. Turn heat to very low and when milk has ceased boiling, cover and cook for about 1 hour, or until milk is almost absorbed. Combine beaten eggs, sugar, raisins and vanilla. Pour into the rice, stirring slowly until rice begins to thicken. Serve hot, warm or leftover and chilled.

* For non-cajuns, Le Bon Temps means fun or good times.

FIVE POINTS DESSERT

Southwesterners are casual, comfortable and cool except where serious eating is concerned. Five Points Dessert is a dazzling five layers of good things direct from New Mexico.

Yield: About 12 servings

I.

1 cup all-purpose flour   1 cup chopped pecans
1 stick margarine

II.

8 oz. bar cream cheese at   1 cup whipped cream
   room temperature   substitute (from 9-oz.
1 cup Imperial 10X   carton)
   Powdered Sugar

III.

1 small pkg. instant   1 small pkg. instant
   vanilla pudding   chocolate pudding
                                 3 cups milk

IV.
Remainder of the whipped cream substitute

V.

Grated frozen milk   Chopped nuts
   chocolate

Combine ingredients in I, and pat into 9″ x 12″ pan; bake in pre-heated 325-degree oven 30 minutes.

Beat together ingredients in II, and spread over crust.

Combine ingredients in III, beating until thick, and spread over the cream cheese mixture.

Spread remainder of the whipped cream substitute over pudding layer.

Grate frozen milk chocolate over whipped cream substitute and sprinkle with the chopped nuts.

Chill and serve.

STATE FAIR ICE CREAM

State fair time is big business in the Southwest. Ask any young rancher whose prize animal was just auctioned for a king's ransom. State fair time also signifies good food, carnival hawkers, and rodeos. See you at the fair!

Yield: about $1/2$ gallon

4 egg yolks
1 cup Imperial
  Granulated Sugar
¹/₄ tsp. salt
2 cups milk, divided
1 cup heavy cream

1 cup buttermilk
¹/₂ tsp. almond extract
3 cups sweetened,
  crushed peaches, fresh
  or frozen

Beat egg yolks until light lemon colored; beat in Imperial Granulated Sugar and salt. Add 1 cup milk. Cook in top of double boiler over simmering water, stirring constantly, until mixture is thickened. Chill in refrigerator, then add second cup of milk and remaining ingredients. Freeze in a crank-type or electric ice cream freezer, using 1 part rock salt to 8 parts ice. Stores well in freezer without forming ice crystals. To freeze in freezing compartment of refrigerator, freeze until mushy, then beat to break up any ice crystals. Return to freezing compartment until hard.

ATHENS BLUEBERRY KUCHEN

New varieties of blueberries now grow in the Southwest. When you make Athens Blueberry Kuchen, the fruit could be from Athens, Texas.

Yield: 8–10 servings

1 cup plus 2 tbsp. all-
  purpose flour
¹/₈ tsp. salt
1 cup plus 2 tbsp.
  Imperial Granulated
  Sugar
¹/₂ cup butter or
  margarine

1 tbsp. white vinegar
¹/₈ tsp. cinnamon
3 cups blueberries, fresh
  or frozen
Imperial 10X Powdered
  Sugar

Combine 1 cup flour, salt and 2 tbsp. of the sugar; cut in butter to make coarse crumbs and stir in vinegar. Shape pastry into a ball and spread it in 9″ round layer cake pan or springform pan, shaping 1″ up sides of pan. Combine the 1 cup of sugar, 2 tbsp. flour and cinnamon; add this to the blueberries and toss lightly to combine.

Transfer to pastry shell. Bake in preheated 400-degree oven 45 minutes to 1 hour. Cool and remove rim of springform pan, if used. Dust top with powdered sugar.

STONEWALL PEACH TURNOVERS

The Southwest produces some of the best peaches available anywhere, such as Stonewalls from Central Texas.

Yield: 8 pies

¹/₂ **cup shortening**
2 **cups all-purpose flour**
2 **tbsp. Imperial Granulated Sugar**
4 **tsp. baking powder**
¹/₂ **tsp. salt**
²/₃ **cup milk**
2 **cups sliced fresh peaches (or thawed and drained frozen peaches)**

¹/₄ **cup Imperial Granulated Sugar**
¹/₂ **tsp. nutmeg**
3 **tbsp. butter or margarine, melted**
1 **egg, beaten with 1 tbsp. water**
Imperial 10X Powdered Sugar
Peach juice

Work shortening into combined dry ingredients until like coarse meal; stir in milk and shape into a ball. Knead lightly on floured surface a few times. Divide dough into 8 equal pieces and roll each into a circle. Combine remaining ingredients (except egg, powdered sugar, and peach juice) adding 1 to 2 tbsp. flour if needed. Place filling in center of each pastry circle, moisten edges of pastry and fold to make half-moon shaped pies. Crimp edges of pies with fork and brush tops with the egg beaten with 1 tbsp. of water. Bake on ungreased baking sheet in preheated 400-degree oven for about 15 minutes or until golden brown. Make a glaze by combining Imperial 10X Powdered Sugar with peach juice and brush glaze on pastries while they are still warm.

RIVER BOAT RAISIN BREAD PUDDING

Have a late breakfast of orange juice, bread pudding and black coffee while on a leisurely riverboat ride down a lazy river in Louisiana. But don't have a single serious thought until the bread pudding is gone — just dream a while.

Yield: about 6 servings

5 slices day-old raisin bread	$2/3$ cup Imperial Granulated Sugar
$1/4$ cup butter or margarine, melted	2 cups milk or cream
2 eggs, beaten lightly	$1/2$ tsp. vanilla

Line bottom of buttered 1-quart baking dish with strips of raisin bread dipped in the melted butter or margarine. Combine remaining ingredients and pour over the bread. Set dish in a pan of very hot water (2″ deep) and bake in preheated 375-degree oven about 30 minutes or until pudding puffs up and a knife inserted in center comes out clean. Serve with Custard Sauce.

Custard Sauce:

$1^1/2$ cups milk	2 tbsp. all-purpose flour
Pinch of salt	$1/2$ tsp. vanilla or almond flavoring
3 egg yolks	
3 tbsp. Imperial Granulated Sugar	

Heat milk almost to boiling; combine remaining ingredients, except flavoring, and stir in some of the hot milk. Return everything to pan of hot milk and cook, stirring, until thickened; do not boil. Stir in flavoring. Serve warm over warm bread pudding.

APPLEBY APPLE DUMPLINGS

Whatever happened to good ole apple dumplings? Here they are, for nostalgic, appreciative appetites. Use crisp, tart cooking apples; add lemon juice for extra flavor.

Yield: about 4 servings

1 cup all-purpose flour
1 tsp. baking powder
1/2 tsp. salt

1/4 cup plus 2 tbsp.
     shortening
1/4 cup milk

Cut shortening into dry ingredients; add milk and blend with fork. Let rest a few minutes. Roll out 1/4" thick on lightly floured surface and cut into 3" x 1" strips.

Apple Mixture:

1 cup Imperial
   Granulated Sugar
2 tbsp. all-purpose flour
1/8 tsp. each nutmeg and
   cinnamon
1 tbsp. fresh lemon juice

1/4 cup water
3 tart apples, peeled,
   cored and sliced
Heavy cream, whipped
   cream or vanilla ice
   cream

Combine dry ingredients in medium saucepan and stir in liquids. Add apples and cook, stirring, until mixture is boiling and beginning to thicken. Gently drop in pastry strips, then transfer to deep casserole. Bake in preheated 350-degree oven for about 35 minutes, or until browned and puffed up. Delicious either hot or chilled. Serve with cream, whipped cream or ice cream — or just plain.

CHRISTMAS TREE LOG

In the Southwest, a Christmas tree may be in the middle of the oil patch. But this one goes in the middle of the Christmas dinner table to delight young and old.

Yield: about 6 servings

1 tsp. cocoa powder
1 tbsp. Imperial 10X
   Powdered Sugar
1/2 pint (1 cup) heavy
   cream for whipping

18 thin chocolate wafers
Additional Imperial 10X
   Powdered Sugar

Combine cocoa powder, sugar and cream and whip until stiff

enough to stand in peaks. Using about half of the chocolate cream, spread cream on one side of each cookie and stack together to make a long roll. Wrap the cookie roll in foil or plastic wrap and chill; refrigerate remaining chocolate cream. Just before serving, unwrap the roll and place it on a serving platter. Cover the roll with remaining chocolate cream; make ridges in the frosting to look like tree bark. Sprinkle with powdered sugar, decorate with chocolate curls and sprigs of holly, if desired.

This is good anytime — not only during the holidays.

NEW LONDON TRIFLE

Trifle is a natural for the Southwest. The fruits and dairy products, from local producers, are put together with plain cake and jam. Our British cousins taught us this one.

Yield: 8 servings

2 cups milk
1 cup Imperial
   Granulated Sugar
1 tbsp. cornstarch
1/4 tsp. salt
4 egg yolks, beaten
1 tsp. vanilla
12 ladyfingers or stale
   pound cake (cut in
   strips)

Raspberry jam
Dry Sherry, optional
Drained fruits, fresh,
   canned or frozen
1/2 pint (1 cup) heavy
   cream, whipped
Maraschino cherries

Heat milk until almost boiling; with pan off heat, stir in combined dry ingredients. Return to heat and bring to boiling, stirring. Pour some of hot mixture over beaten egg yolks, then pour egg mixture into saucepan and heat almost to boil, stirring. Stir in vanilla. Cover custard with plastic wrap and cool, then chill in refrigerator. Spread ladyfingers or cake strips with raspberry (or your favorite) jam or preserves; arrange them in bottom and around sides of a glass bowl. Sprinkle sherry over them. Layer the fruits, custard, and whipped cream over the cake and top with whipped cream and cherries. Garnish attractively.

ORANGE CHIFFON MOUSSE

Citrus groves of South Texas provide the key ingredient in Orange Chiffon Mousse. Valley oranges and grapefruit also provide the morning sunshine on Southwesterners' breakfast tables.

Yield: 6 servings

1 (6-oz.) can frozen
   orange juice, thawed,
   no water
1 tbsp. fresh lemon juice
2 tsp. unflavored gelatin
3/4 cup plain non-fat
   yogurt

2 egg whites, at room
   temperature
Pinch of salt
1/4 cup Imperial
   Granulated Sugar
1 cup heavy cream,
   whipped

Combine juices and gelatin in small saucepan and let stand 10 minutes. Set over low heat and stir until gelatin dissolves. Pour into bowl and stir in yogurt. Set bowl in larger bowl half filled with ice cubes and cold water. Stir until mixture begins to thicken but is not set (or refrigerate for about 45 minutes, stirring occasionally).

   Beat egg whites with salt to soft peaks; gradually beat in sugar until egg whites are stiff but not dry. Fold spoonful of egg whites into orange mixture to lighten, then spoon orange mixture over whites and fold in. Serve mousse in stemmed crystal glasses. Chill. At serving time, top with whipped cream. Can be prepared 1 day ahead, if desired.

HIGH-TECH RICE PUDDING

Here is state-of-the-art rice pudding, so we call it High-Tech. It's way out front of other rice puddings — it will remind you of a certain Southwestern university that's home to intellectuals.

Yield: 8 servings

2 cups milk
²/₃ cup Imperial
   Granulated Sugar
¹/₄ tsp. salt
¹/₄ cup all-purpose flour
1 tsp. vanilla
¹/₂ tsp. cinnamon
2 eggs, beaten
¹/₃ cup currants or white
   raisins

¹/₂ cup pineapple
   preserves
2¹/₂ cups freshly cooked
   rice
¹/₄ cup chopped
   maraschino cherries
¹/₃ cup flaked coconut
¹/₃ cup chopped pecans

Heat milk to boiling; remove from heat and stir in mixture of sugar, salt and flour. Return to heat and bring to boil; stir a small amount of hot pudding into vanilla, cinnamon and beaten eggs, then pour eggs into pudding, stirring over low heat until thickened. Stir in remaining ingredients and let cool, then chill in 8 serving dishes such as parfait glasses. Top with whipped cream, if desired.

SICILY'S BISCUIT TORTONI

Italian cuisine is more than pasta, more than pizza and pesto. Biscuit Tortoni is a welcome light sweet inspired by Sicily, Louisiana.

Yield: 6–8 servings

2 eggs, separated
¹/₂ cup Imperial 10X
   Powdered Sugar
2 tbsp. sherry or rum
¹/₂ tsp. vanilla

1 cup heavy cream,
   whipped
³/₄ cup crushed
   macaroons, divided
¹/₄ cup maraschino
   cherries, chopped and
   drained

Beat egg yolks with the sugar until fluffy and light lemon color. Stir in the sherry or rum and vanilla. Beat egg whites until stiff and peaked. Fold egg yolk mixture into beaten egg whites; fold in whipped cream. Stir in ¹/₂ cup of the crushed macaroons and the cherries. Put mixture in individual ramekins, sherbet dishes or paper muffin cups. Sprinkle each with remaining macaroon crumbs. Freeze until firm.

PORT OF CALL FRENCH DONUTS

*Just once, stroll down to the market, early in the morning, in New Or-
leans. Order the beignets and the wonderful coffee laced with chicory.
Unforgettable. Watch the people and listen to the sounds of a great port
city waking up.*

Yield: about 3 dozen donuts

3 cups all-purpose flour	1/4 cup cooking oil
1 pkg. dry yeast	3/4 tsp. salt
1/2 tsp. ground nutmeg	1 egg, beaten to blend
1 cup milk	Fat for deep frying
1/4 cup Imperial Granulated Sugar	Sugar Glaze

Combine 1¹/₂ cups flour, the yeast and nutmeg. Combine milk,
sugar, oil and salt; heat until warm. Add liquid to dry ingredients
and stir in egg. Beat at low speed with electric mixer for 30 seconds.
Beat 3 minutes at high speed. By hand, stir in remaining flour to
make a soft dough. Place dough in greased bowl and turn once.
Cover and chill. Place dough on lightly floured surface, cover and let
rest 10 minutes. Roll dough to 18 x 12-inch rectangle. Cut into
donut shapes. Cover again and let rise 30 minutes. Fry in deep, 375-
degree F. fat until golden, turning once. Drain and drizzle with
Sugar Glaze.

Sugar Glaze:

To 2 cups Imperial 10X Powdered Sugar add 1 tbsp. melted butter
or margarine, ¹/₂ tsp. vanilla and enough milk to make a thin glaze.

NOTE: Nothing is quite so good as fresh, homemade donuts, but
when there is not enough time to make them, try deep-frying canned
biscuits. Using a 1″ cutter or your thumb, remove the center and fry
and glaze as above. Deliciously easy.

SOUTH OF SOUTHWEST CUSTARDS

Custard or flan is a classic Mexican dessert that's loved the world over. It's best served with a caramel sauce. Delicate, creamy and comforting.

Yield: 6–8 servings

2 cups light cream
¹/₂ cup Imperial
   Granulated Sugar

6 egg yolks
2 tsp. vanilla

Scald cream and sugar in saucepan; cool to lukewarm. Beat egg yolks until thick and lemon colored. Add vanilla to the cream mixture and add in a stream to the beaten eggs, stirring to combine well. Pour into 6 to 8 custard cups and cover with lids or foil. Place in a baking pan, add hot water halfway up outsides of custard containers and bake in center of preheated 350-degree oven 25 minutes or until custards are set. Let cool completely, uncovered, then chill. Serve with a fresh strawberry or raspberry sauce.

Pies

XIT CREAM CHEESE AND MINCEMEAT PIE

Mincemeat was a favorite during early ranching days when outdoor life created hearty appetites. Modern mincemeat pie is tamed a bit with cream cheese.

Yield: 1 9″ pie

4 3-oz. pkgs. cream
   cheese
¹/₂ cup Imperial
   Granulated Sugar
2 eggs, beaten
1 tbsp. lemon rind, grated
1 tbsp. lemon juice

2 cups mincemeat
1 9″ baked pastry shell
1 cup sour cream
¹/₂ tsp. vanilla
2 tbsp. Imperial
   Granulated Sugar

With cream cheese at room temperature, add $^1/_2$ cup sugar, beaten eggs, lemon rind and lemon juice; beat until smooth. Carefully spoon mincemeat into baked pie shell. Spread cream cheese mixture evenly over the mincemeat. Bake in preheated 375-degree oven for 20 minutes. Remove from oven and cover with mixture of sour cream, vanilla and 2 tbsp. sugar. Bake 10 minutes longer. Cool, then chill before serving.

MOUNTAIN HOME CHOCOLATE COCONUT PIE

After boating on Twin Lakes all afternoon, relax with a delicious Arkansas chocolate dessert.

Yield: 1 10″ pie

4 oz. sweet baking chocolate	**3 tbsp. cornstarch**
$^1/_4$ cup butter or margarine	**$^1/_8$ tsp. salt**
$1^2/_3$ cups ($13^1/_2$ oz.) evaporated milk or light cream	**2 eggs, lightly beaten**
	1 tsp. vanilla
	1 10″ unbaked pastry shell
$1^1/_2$ cups Imperial Granulated Sugar	**$1^1/_3$ cups shredded coconut**
	$^1/_2$ cup pecans, chopped

Melt chocolate and butter or margarine in top of double boiler over hot water, stirring to blend. Remove from heat and gradually stir in milk. Combine sugar, cornstarch, salt, beaten eggs and vanilla; blend in chocolate mixture. Pour filling into pastry shell and sprinkle combined coconut and pecans over filling. Bake in preheated 375-degree oven 45 minutes or until center of pie is puffed up; filling will be soft. Chill thoroughly, about 4 hours, before serving. Cut this rich pie into small wedges to serve 10 or 12.

LAFAYETTE STRAWBERRY PIE

From Shreveport to New Orleans, from Lake Charles to Baton Rouge, Fluffy Strawberry Pie is in everybody's fridge.

Yield: 8 servings

Crust:

1¹/₂ cups fine vanilla
wafer crumbs

¹/₃ cup butter or
margarine, melted

Filling:

1³/₄ cups milk
1 cup Imperial 10X
Powdered Sugar,
unsifted

¹/₄ tsp. salt
¹/₄ cup all-purpose flour
1 large egg, beaten
1 tsp. vanilla

Topping:

1 cup strawberry slices,
sweetened and drained
(fresh or frozen)

1 cup heavy cream,
whipped, or substitute

For crust, mix all but 2 tbsp. crumbs with melted butter or margarine; press into buttered 9″ pie pan; chill until firm, about 30 minutes. For filling, heat milk almost to boiling over moderate heat; remove from heat and while stirring with wire whip, add mixture of sugar, salt and flour. (To measure sugar for this recipe, spoon into 1-cup measure until level without packing.) Return to heat and stir until mixture begins to boil. Beat egg and vanilla together and add some of hot liquid to egg, stirring well. Pour egg mixture into filling and heat while stirring about 15 seconds or until almost boiling. Pour filling into bowl and cover with plastic wrap to cool, then chill. Transfer filling to pie crust. For topping, drain strawberries well and put between paper towels to absorb excess moisture. Fold berries into very thick whipped cream and spread over filling. Sprinkle reserved crumbs over top of pie. Chill for several hours before serving.

NOTE: A 9-oz. pkg. of vanilla wafers makes 3 cups crumbs; a 10-oz. pkg. frozen strawberries makes about 1 cup thawed berries.

RANGE COUNTRY BUTTERMILK PIE

In days of yore, it was not unusual to run out of baking ingredients. In that case, cooks made buttermilk pie or vinegar pie from staples. Now, we make them because they're so good.

Yield: 1 9″ pie

1³/₄ cups Imperial
   Granulated Sugar
¹/₄ cup all-purpose flour
¹/₂ tsp. salt
¹/₂ cup butter or
   margarine, melted

3 eggs, beaten
¹/₂ cup buttermilk
1¹/₂ tsp. vanilla
1 9″ unbaked pastry shell

Combine sugar, flour and salt; add melted butter or margarine and
beaten eggs; beat slightly. Stir in buttermilk and vanilla, beating to
blend well. Pour into unbaked pastry shell and bake in preheated
350-degree oven 45 to 50 minutes. Let cool before cutting.

GRANNY SMITH'S APPLE PIE
WITH CHEDDAR CHEESE

*Once, Granny Smith meant the Smith family grandma; today, it usually
means a good pie apple, perhaps from Smithville, but surely made with
Granny Smith apples.*

Yield: 1 9″ pie

¹/₃ cup Imperial Brown
   Sugar
6–7 cups Granny Smith
   apples, pared, cored
   and thinly sliced
3 tbsp. all-purpose flour
2 tbsp. lemon juice
1 tsp. cinnamon
¹/₂ tsp. nutmeg

1 unbaked 9″ pastry shell
¹/₂ cup Imperial Brown
   Sugar
²/₃ cup Cheddar cheese,
   grated
¹/₂ cup all-purpose flour
¹/₃ cup butter or
   margarine

Combine brown sugar, apple slices, flour, lemon juice, cinnamon
and nutmeg; arrange in unbaked pastry shell. Combine brown
sugar, grated cheese and flour; cut in butter or margarine and sprinkle over apples. Bake in preheated 425-degree oven 40 to 45 minutes
or until apples are tender, covering with foil tent if pastry edges
brown too rapidly. Serve warm with wedges or thin slices of Cheddar cheese.

NOTE: Any tart cooking apple may be substituted or canned, sliced pie apples may also be used.

GARDEN DISTRICT CHOCOLATE DREAM PIE

When in New Orleans, do as the natives do — slow down, cool off and enjoy life over a slice of perfect chocolate pie.

Yield: 1 9" pie

1 9" graham cracker crumb crust
1 tbsp. unflavored gelatin
1/4 cup cold water
1/4 cup boiling water
3 eggs, separated
3/4 cup Imperial Granulated Sugar

1 cup whipping cream
1 tbsp. rum flavoring or 1/4 cup rum
1/2 oz. bittersweet chocolate
1/4 cup cocoa

Make and chill crust. Soak gelatin in cold water 5 minutes. Pour boiling water over softened gelatin, stirring until dissolved. Beat egg yolks till thick and light; add sugar and cocoa; stir till sugar is dissolved. Then stir in dissolved gelatin, blending well. Chill till mixture begins to thicken. Whip cream; fold into chilled mixture. Beat egg whites till stiff and fold into gelatin mixture. Slowly fold in rum and pour into crumb crust; shave chocolate over top of pie. Chill 3 to 4 hours.

CELESTE CHOCOROON PIE

Celeste Chocoroon Pie is as heavenly to eat as its name suggests. Look for Celeste, Texas, near the Oklahoma border.

Yield: 1 9" pie

3 squares unsweetened baking chocolate
1/2 cup (1 stick) butter
3 eggs, beaten
3/4 cup Imperial Granulated Sugar
1/2 cup all-purpose flour

1 tsp. vanilla
2/3 cup sweetened condensed milk (not evaporated milk)
2 2/3 cups shredded coconut

Melt chocolate and butter in saucepan over low heat; stir in beaten eggs, sugar, flour and vanilla. Pour into greased 9″ pie pan. Combine condensed milk and coconut and spoon over chocolate mixture, leaving a ¹/₂″ to 1″ border without coconut. Bake in preheated 350-degree oven for 30 minutes. Cool on rack. If desired, top with whipped cream and drizzle with fudge sauce which can be as easy as melting chocolate morsels.

LA LUZ APPLE CRUMB PIE

There's apple pie, then there's APPLE PIE. This one will "light" up your life.

Yield: 1 9″ pie

6–8 **tart cooking apples**
     or 5 cups canned, sliced
     pie apples
1 **cup Imperial**
     Granulated Sugar,
     divided
1 **tsp. cinnamon**

1 **9-inch pastry shell,**
     unbaked
³/₄ **cup all-purpose flour**
¹/₃ **cup butter or**
     margarine
Buttered Rum Sauce

Pare and core apples, cut in eighths and toss with combined ¹/₂ cup sugar and the cinnamon. Arrange apples in pastry shell. For crumb topping, combine ¹/₂ cup sugar with the flour and cut in butter or margarine until crumbly; sprinkle crumbs over apples. Bake in preheated 400-degree oven about 40 minutes or until apples are done. Serve with warm Buttered Rum Sauce.

Buttered Rum Sauce:

6 **tbsp. butter or**
     margarine
¹/₄ **cup light corn syrup**
³/₄ **cup Imperial Brown**
     Sugar

¹/₂ **tsp. rum flavoring or 2**
     tbsp. rum
1 **tsp. nutmeg**
1 **tsp. orange rind, grated**
1 **cup heavy cream or**
     evaporated milk

In saucepan, combine butter or margarine, corn syrup, and brown sugar and cook over medium heat, stirring, until sugar is dissolved. Stir in remaining ingredients. Blend and serve, warm, over hot apple pie.

LOS FRESNOS LEMON PIE

Classic is something that has passed all the tests and just keeps on setting new records. Lemon pie and Padre Island are like that.

Yield: 1 pie

1 cup Imperial
    Granulated Sugar
1/4 cup all-purpose flour
4 eggs
1 cup light corn syrup

4 tsp. butter or
    margarine, melted and
    cooled
1 lemon, juice and grated
    rind
1 pastry shell, unbaked

Combine sugar and flour; set aside. Beat eggs well and blend in remaining ingredients, then the sugar-flour mixture. Mix well. Pour filling into unbaked pastry shell and bake in preheated 425-degree oven for 10 minutes; reduce heat to 350 degrees and bake another 30 minutes, or until center of pie is puffed up (it will deflate upon cooling).

VARIATIONS: For a completely different flavor, substitute honey for the corn syrup and omit lemon juice; or, omit lemon juice and add 1 cup chocolate morsels, melted; or, substitute 2 tbsp. peanut butter for the butter or margarine and omit lemon juice.

SCOTLAND'S BUTTERSCOTCH ANGEL PIE

This wonderful butterscotch pie comes as close to heaven as you are likely to be on earth, but try Scotland, Arkansas.

Yield: 10–12 servings

4 egg whites
1/4 tsp. cream of tartar
1 cup Imperial
    Granulated Sugar
1 cup Imperial Brown
    Sugar, packed
1/4 cup evaporated milk
    (undiluted)

1/4 cup light corn syrup
1/4 cup butter or
    margarine
1/4 tsp. salt
1 cup heavy cream,
    whipped
1/4 cup cashew nuts,
    chopped (optional)

Beat egg whites and cream of tartar together until frothy. Gradually beat in granulated sugar a little at a time until very stiff and glossy and not grainy. Spread meringue on a 9-inch circle of brown paper or baker's parchment on a baking sheet. Bake in preheated 275-degree oven for 1 hour. Turn off heat and leave meringue in oven until cool or overnight. To make the butterscotch sauce, combine the brown sugar, evaporated milk, corn syrup, butter and salt in saucepan and bring to boil; cook for 3 minutes and cool. For topping, whip the cream.

To assemble: Carefully remove meringue from paper and place on serving plate; drizzle the butterscotch sauce over the meringue and top with the whipped cream. Chill thoroughly. Sprinkle with chopped cashew nuts just before serving. Servings are small, since it is very rich.

OAK CREEK CANYON COBBLER

Pioneer cooks loved to make cobblers for the same reasons we do — they're so simple to make and they please everybody. Peach cobblers are the best, except for cherry!

Yield: 8–10 servings

2 cups (29-oz.can) sliced
    peaches, drained
3 tbsp. lemon juice
1 cup Imperial Brown
    Sugar
1 tsp. cinnamon
3/4 cup all-purpose flour

1/2 cup Imperial
    Granulated Sugar
2 tsp. baking powder
1/4 tsp. salt
3/4 cup milk
1/3 cup butter or
    margarine, melted

Arrange peaches (can be fresh or frozen) in 10″ square baking pan; pour on lemon juice; spread brown sugar and cinnamon over peaches. Combine flour, granulated sugar, baking powder and salt; add milk and stir until smooth. Batter will be thin. Pour batter over peaches and brown sugar. Drizzle melted butter or margarine over batter. Bake in 350-degree oven about 35 minutes.

ANGEL FIRE CHOCOLATE ANGEL PIE

Light up everyone's evening after skiing all day at Angel Fire, New Mexico, with this chocolate pie.

Yield: 1 9″ pie

1 **Meringue shell (see Butterscotch Angel Pie)**
2 **cups semi-sweet chocolate pieces**
1 **tbsp. instant coffee**
1/4 **cup boiling water**
1 **cup heavy cream**
1 **tsp. vanilla**

Melt the chocolate in top of double boiler over hot, not boiling, water. Stir in coffee and boiling water (or 1/4 cup very hot perked coffee). Beat until very creamy and somewhat cooled. Beat the cream until stiff and fold into chocolate gently but thoroughly. Stir in vanilla and pour into cooled meringue shell.

EL CAPITAN PECAN PIE

You don't have to be born in the Southwest to be a native — you can join the club after the second week by learning the language and mastering the cuisine. Start with this pecan pie.

Yield: 1 9″ pie

1 1/2 **cups Imperial Brown sugar, packed**
1/2 **cup Imperial Granulated Sugar**
1/4 **cup water**
2 **tbsp. all-purpose flour**
1/2 **tsp. salt**
2 **eggs, beaten**
1/2 **cup evaporated milk or light cream**
1 1/2 **cups pecan halves**
3/4 **tsp. vanilla**
1 **9″ unbaked pastry shell**

Combine first five ingredients in small bowl and mix well. Beat in eggs. Add milk or cream and mix well. Stir in pecan halves and vanilla. Turn into unbaked 9″ pastry shell. Bake in preheated 400-degree oven for 10 minutes. Reduce heat to 350 degrees and bake an additional 35 to 40 minutes, or until filling is puffed in center and is well browned. Let pie cool before cutting.

NOTE: When baking pies, cover loosely with a tent of foil if pie crust is browning too rapidly.

WEST TEXAS PUMPKIN PIE WITH NUT TOPPING

When the frost is on the punkin, that's time to make a punkin pie. If you can wait that long. Actually, pumpkin pie is now a year-round staple, and there are folks who can't wait for lunch to have it — they eat it for breakfast!

Yield: 1 9″ or 10″ pie

$3/4$ cup Imperial Brown
     Sugar, packed
1 tbsp. all-purpose flour
$1/2$ tsp. salt
$1^1/2$ tsp. cinnamon
$1/2$ tsp. each allspice,
     cloves and ginger

2 cups (1 pound can)
     solid-pack pumpkin or
     fresh-cooked
$1^1/3$ cups evaporated milk
     or light cream
1 egg, beaten slightly
1 Unbaked 9″ or 10″
     pastry shell

Combine and mix well the brown sugar, flour, salt and spices. Stir in the pumpkin, cream or milk and egg, stirring until smooth. Pour into pastry-lined pie pan. Bake in preheated 375-degree oven for 30 minutes, covering with a foil tent if necessary to prevent overbrowning of crust. Remove from oven and add nut topping in a 2″ ring around inside edge of pie. Continue to bake another 15 minutes or until pie puffs up in middle and tests done when a table knife is inserted in middle. Let pie cool on rack and serve with a mound of whipped cream inside the ring of nut topping.

Nut Topping:

1/2 cup pecans, chopped   1 1/2 tsp. orange rind,
1 tbsp. shortening   grated
2 tbsp. Imperial Brown   1 tbsp. all-purpose flour
   Sugar

Combine all ingredients and mix until crumbly.

Pastry Shells

The crust has got to be as good as the filling or it will be left, sadly, on the plate. Here are several winners that will never be left behind.

GRAHAM CRACKER CRUST

It's a long way from Graham, Texas, to where graham crackers are made. We'll give folks in Graham credit anyway for this delicious pie crust.

Yield: 1 pastry shell

2 tbsp. Imperial   1 1/2 cups graham cracker
   Granulated Sugar   or cookie crumbs
1/3 cup butter or
   margarine, melted

Combine ingredients well and press into pie pan. Chill. Chocolate cookie or gingersnap crumbs may be substituted for graham cracker crumbs.

PRESS-APPLY PASTRY SHELL

Southwesterners have inherited resourcefulness from frontier ancestors. No wonder this pastry recipe was invented by a Southwestern cook out of a need to save time and energy.

Yield: 1 pastry shell

1¹/₂ cups all-purpose   ²/₃ cup shortening
    flour   3 tbsp. cold water
¹/₂ tsp. salt

Combine flour and salt; cut in shortening until texture of coarse meal. Gently mix in water with fork. Gather pastry into a ball and press into 9″ pie pan with fingertips, shaping edge decoratively. To bake unfilled, prick dough on sides and bottom with fork (to prevent puffing while baking) and bake in preheated 400-degree oven about 12 minutes or until golden brown.

SALAD OIL PASTRY SHELL

Health-conscious Southwestern cooks will make this pastry using the new light and cholesterol-free oils.

Yield: 1 pastry shell

2 cups all-purpose flour   1¹/₄ tsp. salt
2 tsp. Imperial   ²/₃ cup salad oil
    Granulated Sugar   3 tbsp. milk

Combine dry ingredients in 9″ pie pan. Beat oil and milk together and pour over flour mixture; mix with fork until flour is moistened. Remove about one third of dough for top crust. Press remaining dough evenly in pie pan, covering bottom and sides. Shape edges decoratively. Roll reserved dough into a circle to fit over pie filling. Or, for fruit pie, crumble reserved dough over filling. Bake as pie recipe directs.

TOASTED COCONUT SHELL

You will be reminded of the elegant palm-tree lined boulevards of Galveston when you make this Coconut Pie Shell to dramatize an old pie recipe — just like a weekend in Galveston will spark up your life.

Yield: 1 9″ shell

2 cups flaked coconut   **¹/₄ cup butter or margarine**

Place coconut and butter, mixed together, in 9″ pie pan. Toast in preheated 300-degree oven 15–20 minutes, stirring occasionally, until golden brown. Watch coconut carefully during toasting process since coconut burns easily. Press over bottom and sides of pie pan. Cool before filling. Delicious as a crust for icebox pies.

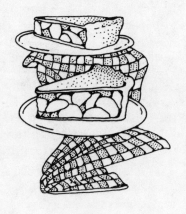

MAIN DISHES

Southwestern "Big Game"

Once upon a time in the Southwest, the phrase "putting meat on the table" meant that the menfolks went into the woods and to the rivers in search of basic foodstuff for their pioneer families — red meat, fish, fowl, and shellfish. This was serious business, not for sport or fun. Life in early Southwestern days meant clearing brush in order to plant crops. Timber had to be cut to build a home. Wool and cotton were spun into yarn then made into cloth to make clothes for mama, papa, grandma, and seven or eight children. Great quantities of food were required to feed the large and hard-working early settlers. Appetites were hearty; food and mealtimes were fundamental.

Until hunters and fishermen returned, no one knew for sure what would go into the kettle or on the spit. Possibilities were quail or wild turkey to stuff and bake; wild duck or rabbit to barbecue; opossum to roast or coon to cook over a campfire and serve with collard greens; or, the most versatile of all, venison for frying, roasting, making into sausage, for stewing or barbecuing.

After cattle was introduced into the Southwest, life was never the same. Wild game was replaced gradually with T-bone steaks and rib roasts from the family herd. Seafood and poultry remained on the menu and currently are challenging traditional red meats. Southwestern cooking retains its unique style with barbecue, chicken-fried steak and chili getting the most votes. But the wide range of ethnic groups that settled the Southwest and the influence from Mexico have spiced up Southwestern foods with irresistible flavors. Note how fajitas and blackened redfish keep appearing on the menu. Chinese, Italian, German, French, Scandinavian and other new Southwesterners have made the region's food as exciting as food anywhere in the world. Choose something good from this modest sampling of what Southwesterners love to come home to eat — food that is fundamental but delicious.

"PIEBOX" RODEO SANDWICHES

Range hand slang for chuckwagon is "piebox," a term filled with both affection and optimism. There was always hope for pie in the chuckwagon. If not, they would just eat more barbecue.

Yield: 4 (¹/₂-cup) servings

¹/₂ **pound ground lean beef**	¹/₂ **tsp. salt**
¹/₂ **cup onion, chopped**	1 **bay leaf**
1 **tbsp. Imperial Brown Sugar**	1 **clove garlic, minced**
2 **tsp. paprika**	1 **cup catsup**
1 **tsp. oregano, crushed**	¹/₄ **cup water**
1 **tsp. chili powder**	1 **tbsp. cider vinegar**
¹/₂ **tsp. cayenne, or to taste**	2 **tbsp. Worcestershire sauce**
	¹/₄ **tsp. liquid smoke, optional**

Brown ground meat in large saucepan in small amount of oil. Add remaining ingredients and combine thoroughly with meat. Bring to boil; reduce heat to low, cover saucepan, and simmer about 15 minutes. Serve on warmed open-face sandwich rolls with onion slices, pickles and mustard, corn on the cob and tall glasses of iced tea.

HOME ON THE RANGE MEAT SAUCE

One interpretation of home-grown is beef — if you live in ranch country. Spaghetti with meat sauce, then, has long been a favorite way to use up the ground beef. Yippee-ti-yo-ti-ya!

Yield: 6 cups

1 cup onions, chopped
2 carrots, peeled and
   shredded
1 clove garlic, minced
$^1/_4$ cup butter or
   margarine
1 lb. lean ground beef
1 28-oz. can whole
   tomatoes
1 6-oz. can tomato paste

$^1/_4$ cup fresh basil,
   chopped or 1 tbsp.
   dried basil
1 tsp. Imperial
   Granulated Sugar
$^1/_2$ tsp. dried oregano
1 tsp. salt
$^3/_4$ cup red wine or tomato
   juice
Hot, freshly cooked rice
   or pasta

Sauté vegetables in butter or margarine in heavy skillet until tender. Add ground meat and brown. Add remaining ingredients, except rice or pasta. Heat to boiling; reduce heat and cook over low heat until sauce is very thick, about 1 hour. Chill thoroughly, then skim off fat and discard. At serving time, heat sauce to boiling and serve over freshly cooked rice or pasta. Sauce may be frozen.

SIERRA BLANCA ZESTY BRISKET

Whether in the mountains of New Mexico or in the rolling hills of Arkansas, this slow-roasted zesty brisket is the easiest way to cook brisket — in the oven.

Yield: about 12 servings

3- to 4-lb. lean brisket or
   boneless chuck roast
Salt and pepper
1 large onion sliced in
   rings

2 large celery ribs
$^1/_2$ cup chili sauce or
   barbecue sauce
$^1/_4$ cup water
1 can beer

Line a large roasting pan with a long sheet of heavy duty aluminum foil with ends long enough to completely cover and seal meat. Place meat on the foil and sprinkle well with salt and pepper. Place onion rings on meat and celery over onions. Combine the chili sauce or barbecue sauce and water and pour over vegetables. Bake uncovered in preheated 375-degree oven about 20 minutes, then pour can

of beer over the brisket; cover and seal tightly with foil. Reduce heat
to 275 degrees and bake 3 to 4 hours. During the last 15 minutes of
baking, open up foil so meat is uncovered; turn heat up to 450 degrees.

TEX-MEX CABBAGE ROLLS

*In the Southwest, we change things around to suit our peppery prefer-
ences. Substitute chili powder and/or cumin for paprika in this old classic.*

Yield: 4 to 6 servings

8 large cabbage leaves	Pepper to taste
1 egg, beaten	1 tsp. chili powder
1/2 lb. ground beef	1 1-lb. can tomatoes
1/4 cup onion, finely chopped	1 8-oz. can tomato sauce
1/4 cup raw rice, regular or instant	Paprika
	Salt and pepper
1/4 cup regular or evaporated milk	Pinch of Imperial Granulated Sugar
1 tsp. salt	1 tsp. lemon juice

Immerse cabbage leaves in boiling water until softened. Combine
meat with remaining ingredients, except tomatoes and tomato
sauce. Roll each cabbage leaf around 1/4 cup of meat mixture, tuck-
ing in ends of cabbage. Arrange rolls, seam side down, in bottom of
ovenproof casserole. Combine tomatoes and tomato sauce and season with additional paprika, salt and pepper to taste, sugar and
lemon juice and pour over cabbage rolls. Bring to boil; cover and
simmer for about 1 1/2 hours.
NOTE: One tbsp. paprika may be substituted for the chili powder.

CANTON EASY CHOP SUEY

*The Chinese, early comers to the Southwest, brought their own cuisine
which has been adopted and adapted in countless ways. Chop suey, they
say, is an adaptation — but a delicious one.*

Yield: 6–8 servings

1 lb. ground beef or
ground turkey
1 cup onion, diced
2 tsp. salt
$^1/_4$ tsp. ground pepper
2 cups celery, thinly
sliced
1$^1/_2$ cups hot water
$^1/_4$ cup red bell pepper,
chopped, or canned
pimiento

1 8-oz. can sliced water
chestnuts
1 #303 can mixed
Chinese vegetables
2 tbsp. cornstarch
2 tbsp. water
1 tbsp. soy sauce
6 cups hot cooked rice

Cook ground beef and onion in skillet until meat loses its red color.
If using turkey, cook about 2 minutes. Add salt, pepper, celery and
1$^1/_2$ cups hot water. Bring to boil, cover and simmer 10 minutes.
Add chopped red pepper or pimiento, water chestnuts and drained
and rinsed canned Chinese vegetables; bring to boil. Blend cornstarch with 2 tbsp. water and stir into mixture. Cook until thickened, stirring. Add soy sauce and correct seasonings. Serve with
freshly cooked hot rice. Sprinkle with toasted almond slivers, if desired.

NOTE: If desired, used fresh bean sprouts, thinly sliced carrots
and/or your favorite mix of vegetables instead of the canned ones.

FORT WORTH MEAT PIES

*Cattle put Fort Worth on the map. Times change, but Fort Worth will
always have its western mystique along with world-class museums and
the wonderful water gardens.*

Yield: 8 meat pies

Pastry:

$^1/_2$ cup shortening
2 cups all-purpose flour
4 tsp. baking powder

$^1/_2$ tsp. salt
$^2/_3$ cup milk (or half milk
and half beef broth)

Cut shortening into combined dry ingredients until crumbly; stir in
liquid with fork and form into ball of dough. Set aside.

Meat Filling:

1 medium potato, diced
1 garlic clove, minced
  and crushed
$^1/_2$ cup onion, diced
$^1/_4$ cup butter or
  margarine, divided

$^1/_4$ cup raisins, optional
1 tsp. salt
Pepper to taste
$^1/_2$ cup beef broth
1 cup beef loin, cubed

Cook vegetables in the butter or margarine until almost done; add raisins, salt, pepper and beef broth; simmer until most of liquid is gone; reserve. In heavy skillet, cook diced beef in 2 tbsp. butter or margarine until beef is lightly browned; combine beef with vegetables. Divide dough into 8 portions and roll each into a 5″ circle. Place about 3 tbsp. of the meat filling in center of each pastry circle; lightly moisten edges of dough and fold dough to make half circles. Press edges of dough together to seal, crimping with tines of a fork. Place prepared pies on ungreased baking sheet and bake in preheated 375-degree oven about 15 minutes, or until nicely browned.

These make delicious picnic fare or school lunches, if they can be kept cold until serving time. Also, if some of the meat filling is not used in the pies, serve it over them as a sauce. Instead of uncooked beef, leftover roast or diced breast of chicken may be substituted.

CAJUN RED BEANS AND RICE

No more are red beans and rice backwoods style. This folksy dish has come to the city. Make red beans and rice at home, using this short-cut method.

Yield: about 8 cups

2 cups diced cooked ham
1 cup each chopped
  celery, onions and
  green pepper
3 bay leaves

1 tsp. each Tabasco sauce,
  black pepper, thyme,
  garlic powder, oregano
  and cayenne pepper
2 qts. water
4 cups canned red kidney
  beans

Put all ingredients, except beans, into a large saucepan or stockpot;

stir well. Cover and bring to a boil. Remove cover and simmer 1 hour, stirring occasionally. Increase heat and cook about 20 minutes, stirring occasionally. Add beans and simmer 30 minutes to 1 hour, stirring occasionally to prevent burning. If beans do scorch, transfer contents of pot to another pot without scraping the bottom of the pan. Discard bay leaves. Taste and add salt, if needed, to suit your taste. Serve over freshly cooked rice.

GALVESTON BUTTERFLY SHRIMP

Think of Galveston; think of sea breezes, surf slamming against the shore, historic homes, lovely bed and breakfast homes, and shrimp boats. Go to Galveston for a seafood holiday, then make these wonderful butterfly shrimp in your own kitchen!

Yield: 4 servings

1 lb. large shrimp, shelled, deveined, tails on
1 egg, beaten
¹/₄ cup each cornstarch, flour and chicken broth
¹/₂ tsp. salt
Oil for deep frying
1 cup each diced green pepper and sliced carrot

1 clove garlic, minced
2 tbsp. cooking oil
1 cup chicken broth
¹/₂ cup Imperial Granulated Sugar
¹/₃ cup cider vinegar
2 tsp. soy sauce
¹/₄ cup water
2 tbsp. cornstarch
Freshly cooked rice

Cut shrimp along outside curve about ³/₄ of the way, press flat and dip in batter made by combining egg, cornstarch, flour, broth and salt beaten until smooth. Fry shrimp in 375-degree F. oil until golden brown, about 5 minutes. Drain and keep warm. In skillet, sauté vegetables until tender but crisp. Add remaining ingredients, except water, cornstarch, and rice, to vegetables and boil 1 minute. Combine water and cornstarch and stir into vegetables. Cook and stir until thickened and bubbling. Arrange hot shrimp over rice and pour sauce over them. If desired, Tabasco or cayenne pepper may be added to the sauce for zest.

NEW ORLEANS SHRIMP CREOLE

Choose New Orleans for a jazzy, magnolia-scented, riverboat, poorboy, Morning Call/beignet kind of retreat to another world. Back home again, make this shrimp creole to stir up those memories of The French Quarter!

Yield: 4 servings

1 lb. shrimp, cooked, shelled and deveined	1/8 tsp. dried thyme
1/2 cup onion, chopped	1 bay leaf
1/2 cup green pepper, chopped	1/2 tsp. Imperial Granulated Sugar
1/4 cup celery, minced	Dash hot pepper sauce
2 cloves garlic, minced	1 tsp. Worcestershire sauce
3 tbsp. butter or margarine	Several whole allspice
1 tbsp. all-purpose flour	Salt and pepper
1 1-lb. can sliced stewed tomatoes	Minced parsley
	Freshly cooked, hot rice

Cook shrimp and remove shells. To make creole sauce, sauté vegetables in butter or margarine until limp; add flour and cook, stirring, until flour is light tan. Add remaining ingredients except parsley and rice and cook until sauce is thickened. Taste for seasonings, adding more if necessary. Stir in parsley. Serve over hot, freshly cooked rice.

OVEN-FRIED CHICKEN AND
GRAVY A LA ALBUQUERQUE

Albuquerque is a blend of Indian, Hispanic, and European cultures. While there, indulge in squaw bread and Indian corn, tortillas and tamales, and chicken and gravy.

Yield: 4 servings

3 lbs. frying chicken cut
  into serving pieces
2 cups milk
1 tsp. salt
2 tbsp. lemon juice

Pinch of cayenne pepper
1 egg beaten with 1 tbsp.
  water
2 cups dry bread crumbs
Oil

Rinse chicken pieces and put in bowl of milk seasoned with salt, lemon juice and pepper; cover and refrigerate 2 hours or overnight. Dip chicken in egg-water mixture, coat with bread crumbs and let stand 10 minutes for coating to set. Place on baking sheet, drizzle with oil, and bake in preheated 350-degree oven about 40 minutes or until golden brown and thoroughly cooked. Serve with mashed potatoes and cream gravy. If preferred, fry instead of bake.

Cream Gravy:

Brown crumbs from baking
  sheet
3 tbsp. butter or margarine
1/4 cup all-purpose flour

1 1/2 cups hot chicken stock
  made from bony pieces of
  chicken
1 cup light cream
Salt and pepper

Scrape any brown crumbs from baking pan into skillet and discard the grease. Melt butter or margarine in skillet over low heat; stir in flour and cook until mixture begins to turn brown. Add hot chicken stock and cream all at once, while stirring. Season to taste.

LITTLE ROCK CHICKEN AND RICE

Call Little Rock eclectic and be right on track. It's the capital city, boasts five museums and two universities, but nobody has yet counted all the churches and schools. Chickens and rice, top Arkansas products, appear often on Little Rock menus.

Yield: 4 servings

1 2 1/2-lb. chicken
1/2 cup cooking oil

1/2 stick butter or
  margarine
Salt and pepper

Split fryer into quarters. Brown chicken in oil and butter in heavy skillet over medium heat until golden brown on all sides. Season with salt and pepper. Place chicken in baking pan; cover with lid or foil and bake in preheated 350-degree oven until chicken is tender and golden brown, about one hour. Serve with Rice and Pecans.

Rice and Pecans:

4¹/₂ cups cooked rice (1¹/₂ cups uncooked)
3³/₄ cups water
1¹/₂ tsp. salt
1 cup pecan halves, toasted in 2 tbsp. butter or margarine

¹/₄ cup parsley, minced
¹/₄ cup onions, diced and sauteed
¹/₄ cup celery, diced and sauteed

Cook 1¹/₂ cups rice in 3³/₄ cups water and 1¹/₂ tsp. salt by your favorite method. When rice is fluffy and water is all absorbed, stir in toasted pecan halves, parsley and sauteed onions and celery using fork to keep rice fluffy.

NOTE: To toast pecans, melt butter or margarine in skillet over medium heat. Stir pecans until they are crisp and beginning to darken. Stir and watch carefully to avoid burning.

SPAGHETTI SAUCE OKLAHOMA STYLE

Take me back to Oklahoma City, seat of state government, home of University of Oklahoma (Norman) and Cowboy Hall of Fame. Oklahoma's hearty, good food includes Mexican, Chinese, down-home and Italian cuisine.

Yield: 8 cups

1 cup onion, chopped
1 clove garlic, mashed
2 tbsp. olive oil or
   vegetable oil
1 lb. ground lean beef
1 cup green pepper,
   chopped
1/2 cup celery, finely
   chopped
2 6-oz. cans tomato paste

2 1-lb. cans whole
   tomatoes
1 tsp. Imperial
   Granulated Sugar
1 tbsp. salt
1 bay leaf
1/4 tsp. each oregano, basil
   and thyme
1/2 tsp. Worcestershire
   sauce

Sauté onion and garlic in oil; stir in meat, breaking it up with a spoon and brown lightly. Add remaining ingredients. Bring to a boil, reduce heat, cover and simmer for about 1 hour, stirring occasionally. Remove cover and simmer long enough to thicken sauce. Serve over pasta cooked to al dente stage. Pass dishes of grated Parmesan cheese and minced parsley.

COUNTRY BOY FRIED FISH

Ask anyone where Bill is; most likely he's "Gone Fishing" in some Southwestern lake or river. But back home is where the fun begins — when the catch is on the table.

Yield: 4 servings of 2 fillets each

4 1-lb. trout (or catfish),
   boned, scaled and cut in
   half
1/2 tsp. salt and dash of
   pepper
1 tsp. lemon juice

2 eggs beaten with 1/2 cup
   milk
1 cup all-purpose flour
2 cups dry bread crumbs
Oil or shortening for
   frying

Rush to the skillet with fresh-caught trout, or choose very fresh fish with bright, clear, bulging eyes; gills that look and smell clean; scales that are shiny and lie close to the skin and with firm flesh that springs back when pressed with fingers. There should be no strong, unpleasant odor. Have your favorite fisherman or butcher bone, scale and cut fish in half. Add salt, pepper and lemon juice to eggs and milk.

Coat fish fillets with flour, dip in egg mixture and coat with dry bread crumbs. Fry in deep fat preheated to 350 degrees F. and cook until crisp and very brown. Transfer to baking sheet and cook in 350-degree oven about 3 minutes. Serve with Tartar Sauce.

Tartar Sauce:

1 cup mayonnaise
1¹/₂ tbsp. pickle relish
1¹/₂ tbsp. parsley, minced
1¹/₂ tbsp. capers, optional

1¹/₂ tbsp. green onions, minced
1¹/₂ tbsp. green olives, minced

Combine all ingredients and chill several hours before serving. Yield: 1 cup. Capers and olives are optional but add unique flavor.

SANTA FE FIERY POT OF CHILI

Visions of La Fonda, the Opera House, pueblos, serranos, serapes, huaraches, tortillas and art galleries portray Santa Fe. If you can't get there this week, make this fiery pot of chili.

Yield: 8 servings

2 lbs. round steak or chuck steak, coarsely ground
¹/₄ cup cooking oil
1¹/₂ cups water or beer
1 8-oz. can tomato sauce
1 cup each onions and green pepper, chopped
6 cloves garlic, minced

1 tsp. oregano
1 tsp. ground cumin
¹/₄ cup chili powder
1 tsp. salt
¹/₂ tsp. Imperial Granulated Sugar
Cayenne pepper to taste
4 medium jalapeno peppers, chopped

In large skillet, brown chili meat in 2 tbsp. of the oil; transfer meat to large kettle, leaving juices in skillet. Add water or beer and tomato sauce to meat and cook over low heat. Sauté vegetables in remaining oil and liquid in skillet. Add remaining ingredients and simmer 30 minutes then add to chili meat in kettle. Simmer about 2 hours. Skim off any excess fat.

ABILENE STEAK WITH WAHOO SAUCE

*Abilene was once the definition of Western, but Abilene has also become
an academic, business, and religious center plop in the middle of cactus
country. Order steak in Abilene or make this version with a peppery
sauce in your own kitchen.*

Yield: 6 servings

6 **Serving size top round steaks, tenderized**	**¹/₂ tsp. chili powder**
1 **15-oz. can tamales, drained (reserve sauce)**	**Dash cayenne pepper**
1 **egg, beaten with 1 tbsp. water**	**Bread crumbs or cracker crumbs for breading**
Flour for breading	**Oil for frying**
Salt and pepper	**¹/₂ cup tomato sauce**
	1 tsp. chili powder
	Dash cayenne pepper

Wrap each steak around a tamale and secure with toothpicks. Dip
steak rolls in beaten egg, then in flour seasoned with salt, pepper,
chili powder and cayenne pepper. Dip again in egg, then in bread
crumbs or cracker crumbs. Brown steak rolls on all sides in the hot
fat; reduce heat, drain off excess fat and cook steaks, covered, until
tender, about 30 minutes. Remove steaks to platter and keep hot.
Add tamale sauce to remaining ingredients and bring to boil. Pour
sauce over hot steaks.

Serving suggestion: Mash two ripe avocados with salt and pepper;
combine with chopped green onion and diced tomatoes. Serve on a
bed of chopped lettuce with crisp corn chips and the steaks.

SIDE DISHES

Those Satisfying Side Dishes

The Southwestern hostess with the most side dishes on the party food table wins the contest for best cook!

And what wonderful side dishes they are — crisp and crunchy salads served with fresh-made tangy dressings, corn soup for a cold winter day, gumbo to eat with fresh-cooked rice, pinto beans or black-eyed peas cooked to perfection.

This section includes a group of casseroles to ensure good eating even on the busiest days. These good foods will solve the problems of what to cook for dinner tonight, what's the tastiest treat to take to the next family party, church supper or what to take to new neighbors on moving-in day. All are designed for delicious eating and sharing which Southwesterners do with gusto.

Casseroles

CATTLE COUNTRY BAKED RICE AND SAUSAGE

Casserole cookery has become more sophisticated — imaginative combinations of ingredients creating economical, filling yet enticing casseroles.

Yield: 4–6 servings

¹/₂ lb. breakfast sausage shaped in 1″ balls
1 medium onion, chopped
¹/₂ cup sliced canned or fresh mushrooms
1 cup uncooked long grain rice

3 cups hot chicken broth
¹/₂ cup frozen green peas
¹/₄ cup diced canned pimiento or fresh red bell pepper
Seasonings to taste

Cook sausage balls and onion in skillet until sausage is lightly browned. Drain off excess fat. Add remaining ingredients and transfer to ovenproof casserole dish; bake in preheated 350-degree oven about 45 minutes. Taste and add salt and pepper, if needed. Added seasonings will depend on seasonings in the sausage and your taste.

OUT WEST CORNBREAD DRESSING

This standard recipe is good as-is, or it can be jazzed up with oysters in bayou country, with jalapeno peppers way out West and with sausage in farm country.

Yield: 10–12 servings

6 cups crumbled
   cornbread
4 cups white bread,
   crumbled
1 cup chopped celery
1 cup chopped onion
$^1/_2$ cup butter or
   margarine, melted

1 tbsp. salt
$^1/_8$ tsp. pepper or to taste
$^1/_4$ tsp. marjoram or sage
1 cup water or milk
4 eggs, beaten, or egg
   substitute
2 cups chicken broth

Crumble breads and reserve. Cook celery and onions in 1 cup water
until tender and add to bread crumbs along with remaining ingredients; mix lightly with a fork. Pour into greased baking dish and
bake in preheated 400-degree oven about 30 minutes or until
browned. Or, stuff a 4–8-lb. chicken or turkey, packing loosely as
dressing swells with roasting.

GREENVILLE RICE AND CHICKEN CASSEROLE

*Broccoli makes this rice casserole green and very good. It appears often
at church suppers, bridge luncheons, and Sunday dinners. And it's nutri-
tious.*

Yield: serves about 6

2 cups cooked rice
2 cups cooked chicken,
   diced
1 10-oz. pkg. frozen
   broccoli flowerets,
   cooked
8 oz. processed cheese
   spread such as Cheese
   Whiz

$^1/_2$ cup (1 stick) butter or
   margarine, melted
$^3/_4$ cup celery, chopped
$^3/_4$ cup onion, chopped
2 cans cream of chicken
   or mushroom soup

Beginning with rice, layer first three ingredients. Combine remaining ingredients and pour over broccoli. Bake in preheated 350-de-
gree oven for about one hour.

ALEXANDRIA ASPARAGUS AU GRATIN

Asparagus Au Gratin is the fairy princess of casseroles whether made from fresh, frozen or canned asparagus. It's perfect for a Louisiana luncheon served with hot rolls and fresh fruit salad.

Yield: 4 servings

1 16-oz. can asparagus, drained (or fresh or frozen)	1/4 cup dry bread crumbs
	2 tbsp. melted butter or margarine
2 cups medium white sauce (see recipe below)	Sprinkle of paprika and/or cayenne
1/2 cup grated Cheddar cheese or diced Velveeta-type cheese	

Arrange asparagus in oval casserole. Make white sauce using liquid from asparagus for part of the milk. Blend cheese into sauce and pour over asparagus. Combine bread crumbs and melted butter or margarine and spread over sauce. Bake in preheated 350-degree oven until sauce is bubbly and bread crumbs are golden brown. Other vegetables such as cooked cauliflower, broccoli, carrots, green beans or green peas could be used.

White Sauce:

1 cup milk or cream	Dash pepper
2 tbsp. all-purpose flour	2 tbsp. butter
1/2 tsp. salt	

Put all ingredients except butter in blender container; blend until smooth; stir in melted butter. Cook over low heat, stirring until thickened.

Yield: 1 cup. For thick sauce, use 2 more tbsp. flour; for thin sauce, use only 1 tbsp. flour.

LEMON SAUCE: Blend an egg yolk with 1 tsp. lemon juice and add to thickened sauce; heat but do not boil.

OTHER VARIATIONS: Stir in minced parsley or pimiento. For a **BROWN SAUCE,** combine flour and butter in saucepan and brown; use beef broth for part of the liquid.

COWPUNCHER PINTO BEANS

The Southwest without red beans is unthinkable — they're the perfect companion for barbecue beef and pork, rice, or grilled chicken, although beans and cornbread are enough for some folks.

Yield: 8 servings

1 lb. dry pinto beans	1 6-oz. can tomato paste
3 qts. water	1 tsp. salt
1/2 pound salt pork, cut up, or ham hock	1/2 tsp. Imperial Granulated Sugar
1 medium onion, chopped	1 tsp. cumin seed
1 clove garlic, minced	1/2 tsp. marjoram

Wash beans and pick over for small rocks or other foreign bits. Place beans in large pot, cover with cold water and soak overnight. When ready to cook, bring beans to boil; reduce heat and simmer 1 hour. Stir in remaining ingredients, cover and simmer 3 hours or until beans are tender. Add more water if necessary and stir occasionally to prevent sticking and scorching. If desired, canned pinto beans may be used; reduce cooking time to about 1 hour. Cornbread is mandatory with this out-West favorite.

Salads

SAN ANTONE CRANBERRY SALAD

There was a time when Southwest food was plain, hearty and simple. Giant strides have been made in variety, quality and creativity of food, and salads are star performers.

Yield: 8–10 servings

1 12-oz. bag fresh
  cranberries
1 lb. green seedless
  grapes
1 8-oz. pkg. miniature
  marshmallows

1 cup chopped pecans
1 cup heavy cream,
  whipped
1 cup Imperial
  Granulated Sugar

Grind cranberries in food grinder or finely chop in food processor; combine with remaining ingredients and chill until serving time.

COLEMAN COLESLAW

This coleslaw isn't strictly for city slickers; everybody likes it. Which goes to show there's a lot of glitz in country folk, too.

Yield: 6 servings

1 3-oz. pkg. lime gelatin
1 cup boiling water
$^1/_2$ cup cold water
1 tbsp. tarragon vinegar
  or your favorite vinegar
$^1/_2$ cup mayonnaise or
  low-fat yogurt

1 cup cabbage, shredded
$^1/_2$ cup carrot, shredded
$^1/_2$ cup celery, slivered
$^1/_3$ cup white raisins,
  optional

Dissolve gelatin in boiling water; add cold water and vinegar and stir until gelatin is dissolved. Gradually stir gelatin into mayonnaise, mixing well. Chill until slightly thickened. Fold in vegetables and raisins and transfer to 6 parfait glasses in order to make coleslaw a conversation piece.

SALADO COMPANY SALAD

Jello salads are well established family and party food in the Southwest. In Salado, Texas, salad is the main part of the town name.

Yield: about 20 squares

2 3-oz. pkgs. lemon jello
3 cups boiling water
1 #2 can crushed pine-
   apple, drained, juice
   reserved
3 bananas, sliced
1¹/₂ cups miniature
   marshmallows
1 cup pineapple
   juice

1 egg, beaten
1¹/₂ tbsp. all-purpose
   flour
¹/₂ cup Imperial
   Granulated Sugar
1 cup heavy cream,
   whipped
1 cup sharp Cheddar
   cheese, grated

Dissolve jello in boiling water; cool. Add pineapple, bananas and marshmallows to cooled jello; chill until firm in 10″ x 13″ pan or glass dish. Heat 1 cup of the pineapple juice over medium heat. Add the beaten egg to the flour and sugar and stir into the pineapple juice off heat; then cook, stirring, until thick; cool. Fold egg mixture into the whipped cream, spread over jello and chill several hours. Just before serving spread grated cheese on top. Cut into about 20 squares.

HIGH FALUTIN' CUCUMBER MOUSSE

Here's a "cool" new twist in cucumbers that makes a welcome summer cooler on the high plains or in high mountains.

Yield: 6–8 servings

2 3-oz. pkgs. lime jello
¹/₂ cup boiling water
Juice of 1 lemon
1 8-oz. carton cottage
   cheese
2 cups mayonnaise (low-
   fat type may be used)

2 tbsp. grated onion
Salt to taste
1¹/₂ medium cucumbers,
   pared, grated and
   drained
¹/₂ cups almonds, slivered

Dissolve jello in boiling water; cool. Stir in lemon juice. Combine remaining ingredients and stir into jello. Wet mold with cold water and add jello mixture. Chill at least 6 hours before unmolding.

MIDWEST CITY FRUIT SALAD

For folks who still like to make mud pies and pottery making is not enough, satisfy your frustrations by making this addictive fruit and cheese salad, mixed by hand.

Yield: 6–8 servings

2 8-oz. bars cream cheese at room temperature	¹/₂ cup coarsely chopped pecans
1 15-oz. can crushed pineapple, well-drained	¹/₂ cup Imperial Brown Sugar, packed
2 cups miniature marshmallows	¹/₂ cup coarsely chopped maraschino cherries, optional
1 15-oz. can fruit cocktail, well-drained	

Combine cream cheese and crushed pineapple; mash with potato masher or use your squeaky-clean hands to thoroughly combine. Add remaining ingredients and combine thoroughly. Pack mixture in serving dish, cover and chill. Garnish attractively with chunks of fruit and pecan halves. This is delicious the first day, but it improves with a day's aging.

RICE PADDY RICE SALAD

Rice is now a major starch food in the Southwest. It's a major crop in Arkansas, Louisiana, and Texas, combines well with other foods and makes terrific salads like this one.

Yield: 4–6 servings

1 tbsp. cider vinegar or
    tarragon vinegar
2 tbsp. salad oil
1 tbsp. prepared mustard
$^3/_4$ tsp. salt
Freshly ground pepper
$2^1/_2$ cups freshly cooked
    long grain rice
$^1/_2$ cup pimiento-stuffed
    olives, chopped

1 hard cooked egg,
    chopped
$^3/_4$ cup slivered celery
2 tbsp. dill pickle,
    chopped
2 tbsp. red bell pepper,
    chopped
3 green onions, chopped
$^1/_4$ cup mayonnaise

Combine vinegar, salad oil, mustard, salt and pepper; stir in hot cooked rice and let stand until cool. Add remaining ingredients and toss lightly. Chill overnight for best flavor. Can be doubled.

ALL-STAR POTATO SALAD

Potato salad, that changeling of countless forms, is the darling of the barbecue spread — suits Astros, Oilers, Cowboys, or Rockets — make it with mustard or not, sweet pickles or dill.

Yield: 4–6 servings

3 medium-size red
    potatoes, well-scrubbed
1 small onion, minced
1 tbsp. fresh parsley,
    minced
$^1/_4$ cup celery, slivered
2 tbsp. green pepper,
    chopped
1 hard-cooked egg,
    chopped

1 clove garlic, minced
1 tsp. creole or Dijon
    style mustard
$^1/_4$ cup mayonnaise
1 tbsp. vinegar
1 tbsp. salad oil
1 tsp. salt
$^1/_4$ tsp. pepper
Hard-cooked egg for
    garnish

Boil well-scrubbed red potatoes in jackets until done in centers; dice, jackets and all, into large bowl. Add remaining ingredients and mix well. Cut the white of the cooked egg into rays of a star and carefully place in center of potato salad; place the yolk in center of egg-white star.

RIO GRANDE DANDY GREEN SALAD

Rio Grande Dandy Green Salad has a style of its own and includes all sorts of green veggies and seasonings. It's a great new addition to the meat, potatoes and coleslaw spread.

Yield: about 6 cups salad

1 cup celery, finely chopped	1 2-oz. jar pimiento, minced
1/2 cup onion, finely chopped	1 1-lb. can French-style green beans, drained
1 green bell pepper, finely chopped	1 1-lb. can small green peas
	1 tsp. salt

Dressing:

1 cup Imperial Granulated Sugar	3/4 cup cider vinegar
1/2 cup salad oil	2 tbsp. water

Combine salad ingredients and gently toss with dressing ingredients. Let stand overnight, covered, in refrigerator. Drain well before serving.

BAYOU SHRIMP AND POTATO SALAD

Just when you thought you knew everything there is to know about potato salad, here comes a shrimp version — the best kind.

Yield: 2 servings

4 medium-size red
  potatoes
2 tbsp. Dijon style
  mustard
1 tbsp. cider vinegar or
  white wine vinegar
1/3 cup olive oil or salad
  oil
3 green onions, chopped

1/2 cup slivered celery
1 tbsp. minced fresh dill
  or 1 tsp. dried dill
Salt and freshly ground
  pepper to taste
1/2 lb. large shrimp,
  cooked, shelled and
  deveined

Cook potatoes in boiling water about 15 minutes or in pressure
cooker about 8 minutes. Pour off hot water and cut in 3/4-inch cubes;
put diced potatoes into large bowl. Combine mustard and vinegar in
small bowl and gradually whisk in the oil; add half of the dressing to
the warm potatoes; stir in green onions, celery and seasonings. Combine shrimp with potatoes and stir in remaining dressing; toss to
coat. Adjust seasonings and serve on crisp greens garnished with
your choice of olives, pickles, plum tomatoes, boiled egg halves or
your choice. Can be doubled.

STUTTGART SAUERKRAUT SALAD

*German sausage is even better when served with Stuttgart Sauerkraut
Salad — a natural combination wherever polkas are playing*

Yield: 8 servings

3/4 cup Imperial
  Granulated Sugar
3/4 tsp. salt
1/2 cup cider vinegar
1/4 cup salad oil
1/2 cup onion, chopped
1/2 cup green or red bell
  pepper, chopped

1/2 cup celery, chopped
1 4-oz. jar pimiento,
  chopped
1 cup unpeeled apple,
  diced
2 cups (1-lb. can)
  sauerkraut, rinsed and
  drained

Combine sugar, salt, vinegar and oil to make dressing. Combine remaining ingredients and toss well with dressing. Chill and drain be-

fore serving. Dressing may be used again in making the next sauerkraut salad.

Salad Dressings

FRENCH SETTLEMENT DRESSING
WITH VARIATIONS

*The Southwest is the land of the individual where everyone likes to make
choices. Even with salad dressings. Here's the opportunity to play
around with different versions of French Dressing for the Southwestern
salad bar.*

Yield: 1^1/$_3$ cups

^{1}/$_3$ cup vinegar or lemon juice	1^1/$_2$ tsp. salt
1 cup salad oil	^{1}/$_2$ tsp. paprika
1 tbsp. Imperial Granulated Sugar	^{1}/$_2$ tsp. dry mustard
	1 clove garlic, minced and mashed

Put all ingredients in tightly closed jar and shake well; chill. Shake
well just before using. Add just enough dressing to coat salad greens
lightly.

JAZZY NEW ORLEANS DRESSING: Add 1 tsp. Worcestershire sauce,
1 drop hot pepper sauce, 2 tbsp. catsup and 1 tbsp. lemon juice to
basic recipe.

SPICY SOUTHWEST DRESSING: Tie 1 tbsp. pickling spices securely
in cheesecloth and add to heated vinegar when making basic recipe
above. When vinegar is cool, remove spices and add to dressing.

DIET FRENCH DRESSING: In making basic recipe, use ^{1}/$_2$ cup oil, 1
tsp. salt and 1 tsp. sugar.

CHEESY CHELSEA DRESSING: Add crumbled blue cheese, Roque-
fort or Stilton cheese.

MINDEN MINTY DRESSING: Add a few sprigs fresh mint to 1 cup of basic dressing and whirl in blender for a few seconds.

OTHER ADDITIONS: Add one or more to basic dressing — pitted green olives, capers, green onions, pickle relish, parsley, anchovies.

CAMPFIRE SALAD DRESSING

When grilling steaks over a campfire under the stars, use this salad dressing for the veggies you'll munch on while the smoke curls upward over smoldering coals.

Yield: About 2¹/₄ cups

1 can tomato soup	1 tsp. dry mustard
¹/₂ cup salad oil	1 tsp. salt
¹/₂ cup red wine vinegar	1 tbsp. grated onion
¹/₂ cup Imperial	1 clove garlic, minced
Granulated Sugar	and crushed
1 tsp. Worcestershire	Bleu cheese, crumbled, if
sauce	desired

Combine all ingredients and whisk to combine. Stir in cheese just before serving.

DIXIE ANN SOUR CREAM DRESSING

Sour Cream Dressing rides the fence — good as a veggie dip for informal cookouts or as a classy green salad dressing for a seated dinner. Stir in some crumbled blue cheese for a Dixieland start-up.

Yield: 1¹/₂ cups

1 cup sour cream or low-	2 tbsp. wine vinegar or
fat yogurt	cider vinegar
¹/₂ cup mayonnaise	¹/₂ tsp. salt
¹/₄ cup chives or green	Dash of pepper
onions, minced	

Combine all ingredients, mix well and chill. This an excellent dip for raw vegetables or crackers.

HAPPY'S SWEET AND SOUR SALAD DRESSING

Tangy, yet sweet, mustard dressing puts a smile on faces all over the Southwest, including those in Happy, Texas.

Yield: about 1 cup

$^1/_3$ cup Imperial
  Granulated Sugar
$^1/_3$ cup prepared yellow
  mustard
2 tbsp. red wine vinegar
  or cider vinegar
$^1/_2$ tsp. salt

$^1/_4$ tsp. freshly ground
  pepper
$^1/_3$ cup salad oil
2 tbsp. water, if needed
$^1/_3$ cup snipped fresh
  dillweed, optional

Whisk together sugar, mustard, vinegar, salt and pepper. Whisk in oil and water if used. Chill. Stir in dillweed just before serving. Delicious on mixed green salads.

SANTA CLARA BLUE CHEESE DRESSING

New Mexico is famous for the blue of Indian turquoise jewelry and blue cheese dressing. Try this favorite version.

Yield: about 2 cups

$^3/_4$ cup wine vinegar
1 tbsp. salt
1 tbsp. Imperial
  Granulated Sugar
$^1/_2$ tsp. hot pepper sauce

$1^1/_2$ tsp. lemon juice
$^1/_2$ cup salad oil
6 oz. Danish blue cheese,
  coarsely crumbled

Combine all ingredients except oil and cheese and mix until sugar is dissolved. Blend in oil with spoon or whisk (not blender or mixer). Fold in crumbled blue cheese. Stir before serving.

Soups

PASEO DEL NORTE TORTILLA SOUP

Tortilla soup is a tempting mix of Tex-Mex flavors that's just right on a chilly, rainy day as well as on a bright, sunny day. Guacamole goes well, and flan makes a sweet, light finish.

Yield: 6 servings

1 small pkg. corn tortillas	$^1/_8$ tsp. ground cumin
Shortening	$^1/_4$ tsp. oregano
2 tomatoes, fresh or	3 tbsp. cornstarch
canned, diced	Grated Monterrey Jack
1 onion, diced	cheese
1 clove garlic, diced and	Fresh cilantro sprigs
mashed	Sour cream, optional
6 cups chicken broth,	
fresh or canned	

Cut tortillas in $^3/_4''$ dice and sauté in small amount of shortening until brown but not crisp. Remove and reserve. Sauté tomatoes, onion and garlic until onions are limp. In large saucepan, combine chicken broth, vegetables, cumin and oregano; bring to boil, lower heat and simmer about 30 minutes. Just before serving, dissolve cornstarch in small amount of water and stir into chicken broth, cooking until thickened. Add tortillas and ladle into heated bowls. Top with the grated cheese, cilantro and dollops of sour cream. For extra excitement, add minced jalapeño pepper. Serve with tostadas.

BAYOU TECHE GUMBO

The mystique is hereby removed from gumbo-making with this authentic, yet simplified version. Hearty and filling, it's a meal when served with rice and followed by dessert.

Yield: 4 servings

2 cups diced cooked
turkey or chicken
2 cups turkey or chicken
broth
2 cups stewed tomatoes
1/2 cup onion, diced
1 tsp. salt

1/2 tsp. gumbo filé
1/2 tsp. Imperial
Granulated Sugar
Dash Black pepper
2 cups sliced fresh or
frozen okra, optional
Freshly cooked rice

Combine all ingredients except okra and rice. Bring to boil. Add okra and cook over medium heat 5 minutes or just until okra is tender. Serve over hot rice or combine with the rice and serve in a bowl as a thick soup.

NOTE: For a spicier version, add a dash of cayenne pepper.

INDIAN VALLEY CORN SOUP

Corn is a winner in Louisiana, and other Southwestern places, whether it's corn on the cob, corn chowder, corn pudding, corn relish or corn soup.

Yield: 8 servings

4 cups chicken broth,
fresh-made or canned
1 cup whole kernel corn,
fresh, canned or frozen
1 tbsp. each green bell
pepper, onion and
celery, chopped

1 cup diced cooked
chicken meat
1 1/2 tsp. salt, or to taste
1/2 tsp. Imperial
Granulated Sugar
Dash cayenne pepper
Egg noodles or rice, if
desired

Combine chicken broth and corn and bring to simmer. Sauté vegetables in small amount of butter or margarine until limp and add to chicken broth with chicken meat, salt, sugar and pepper. Add noodles or rice the last 10 minutes of cooking. Great with regular crackers, oyster crackers or hot French bread wedges.

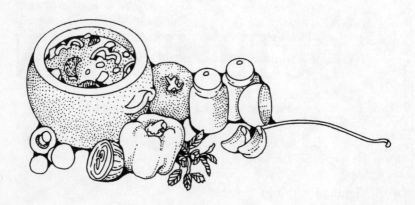

SOUTHWESTERN
SPECIALTIES

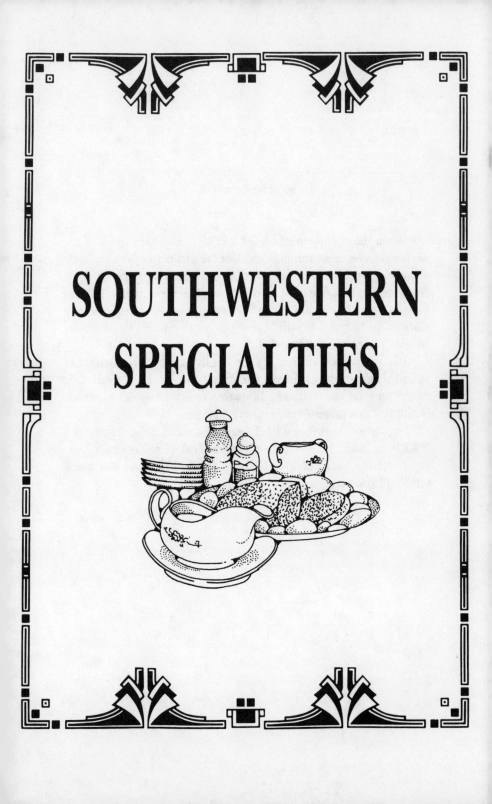

Southwestern Style

When those unfortunate folks who live elsewhere think of the Southwest, they most certainly think of the distinctive Mexican style dishes we love to eat. So this section includes a sampling of some Southwestern adaptations of food from south of the border. If the seasonings are not powerful enough for your palate, go ahead and add more of the hot stuff to satisfy your personal cravings. But don't say we didn't warn you to be careful.

If you have lots of time, do the Brush Country Beef Brisket as an old-timer would. If time is short, make El Rancho Enchiladas; they're so good you won't mind that they're quick and easy to make. Notice that this casserole travels well to parties.

Or, make the Southwest Conference Meat Loaf, Texas Taters, and Wild West Beans for a complete western meal. If you're really hungry, finish the meal with Flan Caramel. Go ahead and see how much fun Southwestern eating can be.

BRUSH COUNTRY BEEF BRISKET
WITH CHUCKWAGON BARBECUE SAUCE

These are the kind of vittles chuckwagon cooks invented to fill up hungry cowboys after a hot, dusty day on the range.

Yield: 8–10 pounds brisket

8–10 boneless beef brisket, packer trimmed

Marinade:

Coarse ground pepper　　**Worcestershire sauce**
Salt　　　　　　　　　　**Liquid smoke**
Paprika

Coat brisket with a mixture of the marinade ingredients. Place meat on grill (fat side up) over hot coals, using charcoal briquets and mesquite chips soaked in water overnight. Close grill and smoke about $1^1/_2$ hours per pound without turning. Add charcoal briquets and mesquite chips as needed but keep heat steady and low. Meat is done when thickest part is no longer pink. To serve, cut away fat, slicing across the grain and serve warm with Chuckwagon Barbecue Sauce. Chop trimmings for sandwiches.

Chuckwagon Barbecue Sauce:

$^1/_4$ cup cooking oil　　　　**1 onion, chopped**
$^1/_4$ cup Imperial Brown　　**$^1/_3$ cup lemon juice**
**　　Sugar**　　　　　　　　**2 tbsp. liquid smoke**
$^2/_3$ cup tomato catsup　　　**$^1/_4$ tsp. pepper**
$^1/_3$ cup water　　　　　　**$1^1/_2$ tsp. salt**
2 tbsp. soy sauce　　　　**1 cup Worcestershire**
1 tbsp. mustard　　　　　**　　sauce**

Simmer combined ingredients over low heat about 30 minutes, stirring occasionally. Yield: 2 to 3 cups. Store in refrigerator until needed; heat gently before using at table with the meat. Marinade can also be used for steaks and other cuts of meat to be grilled.

EL RANCHO ENCHILADAS

This can't-fail version of enchiladas combines with a mariachi band and a group of your best friends to make a fiesta!

Yield: 6–8 servings

1 lb. lean ground beef	1 15-oz. can tomato sauce
1/2 tsp. salt	with jalapeños
2 tbsp. oil	1/2 tsp. salt
2 tbsp. all-purpose flour	12 corn tortillas
2 tbsp. chili powder	2 10-oz. bars sharp
2 cups water	Cheddar cheese, grated
	1 onion, finely chopped

Brown meat lightly, drain off fat and add salt; distribute meat over bottom of 9″ x 13″ baking dish. Cook mixture of oil, flour and chili powder over medium heat about 3 minutes; add water all at once and continue cooking and stirring until sauce begins to thicken. Add tomato sauce and salt and simmer, uncovered, 15 to 20 minutes. Dip each tortilla in hot tomato sauce to soften, then place some grated cheese and chopped onion down middle of each tortilla. Roll them up and place, seam side down, over the layer of meat. Pour remaining sauce over all and sprinkle with the remaining grated cheese and the chopped onion. Bake in preheated 350-degree oven 20 to 25 minutes or until enchiladas are piping hot and the cheese is bubbling.

FAJITAS OLÉ

The secret to making wonderfully tender fajitas is to buy them tenderized. Cuts down cooking time, too. Grill them outside or stir-fry them in your wok.

Yield: about 12 servings

5 lbs. tenderized beef
  skirt steak
1 cup fresh lime juice
4 cloves garlic, crushed
1/4 cup vegetable oil
1 12-oz. can Texas beer or
  next best brand

1 onion, sliced
Salt and pepper to taste
24 flour tortillas
Fixin's: sliced onions,
  chopped cilantro,
  guacamole, picante
  sauce

Have butcher tenderize the meat. Combine remaining ingredients except tortillas and fixin's in non-metallic container (large ziplock bags work well), add meat and toss well to distribute marinade; refrigerate for 24 hours. When ready to cook, grill over a very hot fire, using mesquite if available. Cook about 5 minutes per side, but do not overcook, and baste frequently with marinade. When done, cut meat across the grain in thin strips. Place a portion of meat on warm tortillas, top with a selection of the fixin's and roll tortilla around it all and enjoy.

FLAN CARAMEL

In the Southwest, flan is custard bathed in caramel syrup. It's the perfect ending for a meal of spicy foods — it helps to put out the fire!

Yield: 6–8 servings

1/3 cup Imperial
  Granulated Sugar (for
  caramel syrup)
4 eggs
1/2 cup Imperial
  Granulated Sugar
1/2 tsp. salt

3/4 cup water
1²/3 cups undiluted
  evaporated milk
1 tsp. vanilla
1/4 cup toasted sliced
  almonds, optional

Melt the 1/3 cup sugar over medium heat, stirring, until sugar turns to a golden brown syrup; pour syrup into 1-qt. baking dish or 6 to 8 custard cups. Beat eggs, sugar and salt together; add water, evaporated milk and vanilla, combining well. Do not overbeat to avoid excess air bubbles. Pour custard mixture into mold or cups. Place in pan and pour hot water around mold about 1 inch deep. Bake in preheated 350-degree oven 60 to 70 minutes for 1-qt. mold or about 30 minutes for custard cups or until knife inserted in center of custard comes out clean. Remove from water and cool on rack. Chill until ready to serve. Unmold on platter or on individual dessert plates. Sprinkle with toasted almonds if desired.

SON-OF-A-GUN CASSEROLE

The meaining of "casserole" will never be the same after tasting this one — it's a state-of-the-art, easy-to-make, Tex-Mex dish. String colored lights across the backyard, bring out the sombreros, serapes and this casserole. Sounds like a party!

Yield: about 4 servings

Oil	1 16-oz. can tomato sauce
1 lb. lean ground beef or ground turkey	1 tbsp. chili powder
	1 tsp. salt
1 cup chopped onion	12 tortillas
2 tbsp. minced jalapeño pepper	8 oz. shredded sharp Cheddar cheese

In small amount of oil, lightly brown ground meat; add chopped onion and partially cook. Stir in pepper, tomato sauce and the seasonings. Alternate layers of meat mixture, the tortillas and the grated cheese in buttered 1$^{1}/_2$ quart casserole. Bake in preheated 325-degree oven about 20 minutes. Top with more grated cheese and bake until melted.

SOUTHWEST CONFERENCE MEAT LOAF
WITH PICANTE SAUCE

Southwesterners are friendly, easy-going folks until they choose up sides and root for their favorite team on Sunday afternoon TV. When it's time for food, everyone agrees on Southwest Conference Meat Loaf.

Yield: about 6 servings

1 lb. lean ground beef
1 egg, slightly beaten
1 tsp. salt
¹/₂ tsp. cayenne pepper or
   to taste
1 tsp. lemon juice

¹/₂ cup onion, chopped
¹/₂ cup soft bread crumbs
1 cup canned pinto beans,
   drained
¹/₂ cup tomato catsup
Strips of canned pimiento

Combine all ingredients except catsup and pimiento, mixing lightly. Shape into a football-shaped oval in baking dish. Add 2 tbsp. water to the catsup and drizzle over the meat loaf. Bake, uncovered, in preheated 375-degree oven about 1 hour or until juices run clear and meat loaf is nicely browned. Arrange strips of pimiento over top of meat loaf to lace up the football. Easiest to serve directly from the baking dish.

Touchdown Picante Sauce:

2 cups canned tomatoes,
   including juice
2–4 fresh jalepeño
   peppers

1 onion, coarsely
   chopped
1 clove garlic
Pinch of salt

Process all ingredients in blender until finely chopped. Bring to boil in saucepan, reduce heat, and simmer about 30 minutes. Keeps, refrigerated, about 1 week. Yield: about 2 cups. Serve over everything except ice cream.

HILL COUNTRY TATERS

Southwesterners love to eat, but they especially like zesty food. Meat-and-potatoes folks go for these crusty baked "fries" that are as easy to do as baked potatoes.

Yield: about 4 servings

4 baking potatoes
¹/₂ cup butter or
   margarine, melted

¹/₄ tsp. cayenne pepper
¹/₄ tsp. chili powder
Salt to taste

Scrub potatoes well; dry them but do not peel. Cut each potato into

8 wedge-shaped strips. Each strip will include some peel. Combine melted butter or margarine with seasonings and coat all sides of the potato wedges with the seasoned butter. Arrange the wedges, peel side down, on a baking sheet and bake them in a preheated 400-degree oven about 30 minutes, or until potatoes begin to brown and look puffy. Serve immediately.

WILD WESTERN BEANS

People from other places think the American Southwest is what they see in the old western movies — wild, mean and dangerous. We know better but capitalize on the mystique. Foods like Wild Western Beans help to continue the fun.

Yield: About 8 servings

2 1-lb. cans pork and beans	3/4 cup Imperial Brown Sugar
1 cup onions, chopped	1/2 cup tomato catsup
1/2 cup cola beverage	Salt and cayenne pepper to taste

Combine all ingredients in heavy saucepan; bring to boil then reduce heat to low and simmer 30 minutes to an hour, stirring occasionally. May be baked in 300-degree oven, uncovered, for about an hour.

SECTION INDEX